MANAGING YOU

A selection of other How To books

Buying a Personal Computer
Cash from Your Computer
Creating a Web Site
Creative Writing
Designing for Desktop Publishing
Doing Business on the Internet
Finding a Job in Computers
Finding a Job with a Future
Getting That Job
Getting Your First Job
How to Do Your Own Advertising
How to Do Your Own PR
How to Keep Business Accounts
How to Manage Computers at Work
How to Manage Your Career
How to Market Yourself
How to Master GCSE Accounts
How to Publish a Newsletter
How to Return to Work
How to Start a Business from Home
How to Start Word Processing
How to Start Your Own Business
How to Study and Learn
How to Work from Home

How to Work in an Office
How to Write & Sell Computer Software
Improving Your Written English
Learning New Job Skills
Managing Budgets & Cash Flows
Managing Your Personal Finances
Managing Yourself
Mastering Business English
Planning a New Career
Preparing a Business Plan
Research Methods
Starting to Write
Studying at University
Studying for a Degree
Surviving Redundancy
Taking Your A-Levels
Using the Internet
Winning Presentations
Writing a Press Release
Writing a Report
Writing an Essay
Writing Business Letters
Writing for Publication
Writing Your Dissertation

Other titles in preparation

The How To Series now contains more than 200 titles in the following categories:

Business & Management
Computer Basics
General Reference
Jobs & Careers
Living & Working Abroad

Personal Finance
Self-Development
Small Business
Student Handbooks
Successful Writing

Please send for a free copy of the latest catalogue for full details (see back cover for address).

COMPUTER BASICS

MANAGING YOUR FIRST COMPUTER

How to perform core tasks and gain knowledge and confidence

Carol Dolman and Marcus Saunders

2nd edition

How To Books

Cartoons by Mike Flanagan

British Library Cataloguing in Publication Data
A catalogue record for this book is available from the British Library.

© Copyright 1999 Carol Dolman & Marcus Saunders.

Published by How To Books Ltd, 3 Newtec Place,
Magdalen Road, Oxford OX4 1RE, United Kingdom.
Tel: (01865) 793806. Fax: (01865) 248780.
email: info@howtobooks.co.uk
www.howtobooks.co.uk

First edition 1998.
Second edition 1999.

All rights reserved. No part of this work may be reproduced or stored in an information retrieval system (other than for purposes of review) without the express permission of the Publisher in writing.

Note: The material contained in this book is set out in good faith for general guidance and no liability can be accepted for loss or expense incurred as a result of relying in particular circumstances on statements made in this book. The law and regulations may be complex and liable to change, and readers should check the current position with the relevant authorities before making personal arrangements.

Cover design Shireen Nathoo Design
Cover image PhotoDisc

Produced for How To Books by Deer Park Productions.
Typeset by PDQ Typesetting, Stoke-on-Trent, Staffs.
Printed and bound by Cromwell Press, Trowbridge, Wiltshire.

Contents

List of illustrations		9
Preface		11
1	**Doing useful things with your computer**	13
	Ideas to save and keep	13
	Ways that you can impress people	13
	How the computer can aid learning	14
	Planning larger projects for your home	14
	Things to do for fun	14
	Case study	15
2	**Buying and setting up the computer**	16
	Considering your needs	16
	Looking to the future	16
	Choosing the windows to look through	17
	Types of printers that are available	18
	Putting it together	19
	Turning it on	20
	Case studies	21
	Practical exercise	22
3	**Looking briefly at DOS**	23
	What is DOS?	23
	Understanding the importance of DOS	23
	Looking at two system files	26
	Case study	26
	Practical exercise	26
	Summary	27
4	**Exploring Windows 95/98**	28
	Using a mouse	28
	Where do I begin?	29
	Characteristics of the windows	30

	Personalising the desktop	33
	The icons on your screen	35
	Windows 95/98 accessories	37
	Case study	40
	Practical exercise	40
5	**Exploring Windows 3.11**	**41**
	Where do I begin?	41
	Characteristics of the windows	42
	Personalising the desktop	43
	Creating new windows and icons	44
	Windows 3.11 accessories	46
	Case study	46
	Practical exercise	46
6	**Sorting out drives, paths and trees**	**48**
	Defining drive letter names	48
	Explaining the tree structure	48
	Naming directories/folders and files	49
	Working with the path command	50
	Case study	51
	Practical exercise	51
7	**Understanding your disk drives**	**53**
	Working with floppy disks	53
	Using and playing CD-ROMs	56
	Defining the role of the hard disk drive	57
	Keeping your computer healthy	58
	Case study	60
	Practical exercise	60
8	**Organising your computer with Windows 95/98**	**61**
	Seeing where it is all stored – the explorer	61
	Loading a new program	64
	Adding and removing entries from the menu	65
	Case study	67
	Practical exercise	67
9	**Organising your computer with Windows 3.11**	**69**
	Seeing where it is all stored – the file manager	69
	Loading a new program	71
	Adding and removing icons from the groups	72
	Case study	72
	Practical exercise	72

Contents

10 Looking at programs for correspondence — 74

    Creating letters with word processing — 74
    Improving the layout in an instant — 81
    Designing with desktop publishing — 84
    Adding that special look — 87
    Having your work checked by the spellchecker — 88
    Previewing and printing your work — 89
    Case study — 91
    Practical exercise — 91

11 Looking at programs to calculate with — 93

    Calculating with spreadsheets — 93
    Letting the program do the sums for you — 96
    Home accounting with finance packages — 98
    Being shown your spending habits — 100
    Case study — 101
    Practical exercise — 101

12 Looking at programs to store information — 103

    Building and using databases — 103
    Knowing what databases can be used for — 106
    Keeping a diary with a PIM — 107
    Case study — 108
    Practical exercise — 109

13 Looking at programs for having fun — 111

    Relaxing and learning with games and education — 111
    Encouraging your children to use reference programs — 113
    Improving your hobbies and pastimes — 115
    Case study — 115
    Summary — 115

14 Communicating with the outside world — 116

    Understanding the terminology — 116
    Connecting with a modem — 117
    Setting up a fax/answering machine — 117
    E-mail and the Internet — 118
    Wandering around on the World Wide Web — 120
    Case study — 122
    Practical exercise — 123

15	**Finding even more practical uses**	**124**
	Adding pictures with scanners	124
	Making music	126
	Upgrading your computer	127
	Case study	128

Appendix: Suggested system requirements 130

Glossary 134

Further reading 140

Useful addresses 142

Index 143

List of Illustrations

1	Samples of printers	18
2	Rear view of a system unit	19
3	Sample DOS screen displaying the time	24
4	Task bar with two programs open	29
5	Fly-out menu system	30
6	A window	31
7	A scroll bar	32
8	Screen saver dialogue box	34
9	Sample icons on a desktop	35
10	A help window	38
11	The shut down dialogue box	39
12	Program manager in Windows 3.11	42
13	Pressing the alt and tab keys	43
14	New program object dialogue box	44
15	New program group dialogue box	44
16	New program item dialogue box	45
17	Minesweeper game	47
18	A tree structure	49
19	Floppy disks	53
20	The format dialogue box	54
21	The run dialogue box	55
22	Save as... dialogue box	56
23	Defrag start-up information	59
24	Hard disk properties dialogue box	60
25	Windows 95 explorer window	62
26	Showing the explorer tree structure	63
27	Add/remove programs dialogue box	65
28	Task bar properties box	66
29	Windows 3.11 file manager window	70
30	Copying files from one window to another	71
31	Word processor screen	75
32	The open file dialogue box	78
33	Confirming information dialogue box	79
34	Highlighted text	82
35	Sample icons in programs	83

36	Desktop publishing facilities	85
37	Explaining layers	86
38	Showing picture cropping	86
39	More desktop publishing features	87
40	Spellcheck dialogue box	89
41	Printer dialogue box	90
42	Cell reference in spreadsheets	94
43	Formatting number dialogue boxes	94
44	A selected column	95
45	The adjust cursor	95
46	Different format entries	96
47	Displaying calculation results	97
48	Displaying hidden formulae	98
49	A Quicken financial sheet	99
50	Graphical representation of finances	100
51	A database record	104
52	Enlarging a field	105
53	Selecting records	106
54	Searching for information	107
55	Sample screenshot of an encyclopaedia	114
56	An e-mail being written	120
57	The AOL browser	121

Preface

Welcome to the world of computing.

It doesn't matter who we are, where we live or where we work, computers will affect our lives in one way or another. For many years it was thought that they would go away if we ignored them for long enough but the reality couldn't be more wrong.

The computer industry seems to have difficulty keeping up with itself. This means of course that we at the consumer end of the market have a problem. If we buy a computer system now, within six months it will be well out of date. There's no point in waiting six months to buy the latest technology because the same thing will inevitably happen again. But does all this really matter that much?

The simple answer is no. If you buy a computer then you will have bought it to perform some function or another and, as long as your machine satisfies your needs, why worry about it? If you can resist the impulse to become a 'Power Junkie' then your computing investment will give you a good return.

This second edition of our book has been revised to include the changes that Windows 98 brought to the topics covered in the original, and machine specifications have also been amended.

Knowing more about computers will increase your confidence at work and in many other areas of your life so we wish you well and hope that this book will help you enjoy your computing experience.

Marcus Saunders and Carol Dolman

1
Doing Useful Things with Your Computer

The uses to which a home computer can be put are almost endless. This chapter will give you some basic suggestions as food for thought. A computer by nature is a very dumb machine that is only capable of adding up figures. By installing **software** – another name for **programs** – they become very versatile pieces of equipment that can help you accomplish many things. All the ideas mentioned here can be achieved with the appropriate software installed, and are limited to using popular software that most people can easily acquire. With more specialised programs an awful lot more can be achieved.

IDEAS TO SAVE AND KEEP

- Keep a log of those important reference numbers – passport, insurance and driving licence numbers, credit card and bank account numbers, etc.
- Create a database of your music collection.
- Build up a favourite recipe collection.
- Have your own personal diary and address book.
- Keep an on-going check of your personal finance.
- Remember the Christmas and birthday presents you have given or received.
- Plan your future schedules.

WAYS THAT YOU CAN IMPRESS PEOPLE

- Produce newsletters for your local sport or social club.
- Print your own invitations.
- Send personally produced greeting cards.

- Create a professional looking CV.
- Type impressive job applications.
- Convert important information into tables and graphs for presentations.
- Print headed notepaper and business cards.

HOW THE COMPUTER CAN AID LEARNING

- Help your children learn mathematics and other school subjects.
- Learn a foreign language.
- Play a musical instrument with computer aided learning packages.
- Look up reference from one of the many encyclopaedias available.
- Improve general knowledge with trivia packages and quizzes.
- Use the Internet for Open University degree courses.
- Improve your thinking skills with simulator programs.

PLANNING LARGER PROJECTS FOR YOUR HOME

- Completely redesign your home decor with computer assistance.
- See what your garden will look like in ten years time using a 3D garden designer.
- Work out financial changes and implications with spreadsheets.
- Write a book.
- Design your ideal home with CAD (computer aided design).

THINGS TO DO FOR FUN

- Pass the time with some fun and exciting games.
- Scan the family photographs and manipulate them to give various effects.
- See what a new hairstyle will look like before having it done.
- Surf the Internet and chat to people all over the world.
- Learn to play golf or fly a plane.

Doing Useful Things with Your Computer

- Experience your alter ego with first person adventures.

Hopefully these suggestions will have broadened your outlook on computers and how they may be able to enhance your life. Try to see them not as some mysterious piece of hi-tech equipment to be viewed with caution, but as an exciting development helping you achieve new experiences.

CASE STUDY

Eric is a retired company director and lives with his wife in a converted farmhouse. Part of the house is occupied by their son Mark, his wife Lucy and their two children, Lee aged 6 and Beverly, 13. During the course of this book we will be looking at the family's introduction to computers.

2
Buying and Setting Up the Computer

CONSIDERING YOUR NEEDS

The first question to ask yourself is 'What do I want to use it for?' Looking through the previous chapter may enable you to answer this more accurately and help you decide what sort of system you will require. Some of the more common tasks such as writing letters, keeping financial accounts and playing small puzzle-type games can be accomplished on all types of computer, once the programs are installed. Today there are so many more uses for them that further points should be considered before a choice is made.

What questions should I ask myself?
1. Do I just wish to type letters and very basic things?
2. Will I want to play some of the fast and exciting games available?
3. Do I wish to use reference programs such as encyclopaedias and educational material?
4. Would I like to be able to do work involving graphics and photographs?
5. Would I like to use my computer to access the **Internet**?
6. Will I need to send and receive faxes, or set up an answering machine?
7. Am I interested in recording and playing sound and videos?
8. Will I wish to print out professional looking letters and leaflets?
9. Am I liable to use colour printing often or just occasionally?

LOOKING TO THE FUTURE

When considering your needs, try to think ahead. You may not

Buying and Setting Up the Computer 17

want to use your machine for reference, but will your children or grandchildren? As you become more experienced, you may wish to experiment with other things such as faxes and the Internet so always buy the best you can afford.

Computer systems advance so rapidly that new systems are continually hitting the market and prices of the previous machines drop rapidly. A computer bought for £1,000 today may be purchased for £600 in six months so don't expect your investment to have much of a secondhand value. By buying carefully your needs will not increase at such a rate, so a good machine will last at least a couple of years. Machines can now usually be upgraded at a reasonable cost when it proves necessary.

CHOOSING THE WINDOWS TO LOOK THROUGH

There are three versions of Windows that you may find installed on your computer. If you have purchased second hand, you may have a version including DOS and Windows 3.11. If you have bought a new machine, you will have Windows 95 or Windows 98.

Windows 3.11 advantages
- easy to set up and learn
- takes up a small amount of **hard disk** space
- needs little **memory** to run.

Windows 3.11 disadvantages
- is now obsolete
- some recent programs are not compatible
- requires more user input when adding devices such as **scanners**
- requires a reasonable working knowledge of DOS.

Windows 95/98 advantages
- is easy to use once learnt
- can perform more than one task at a time
- it requires minimal user help when setting up additional devices
- long **file** names can be used enabling better description for saved files
- DOS can be largely ignored.

Windows 95/98 disadvantages
- takes up more than 70 **megabytes** of **disk space**
- requires 16 megabytes of memory to run at satisfactory speed

- can encounter problems when trying to run some DOS programs
- will not work on older machines.

Windows 98 advantages over Windows 95
- a more up to date operating system
- is more interactive with the Internet
- has more effective system tools to keep your machine healthy
- one or two extra features enable easier desktop management.

When choosing which Windows system to use, first consider your machine. If your computer has a 386 or 486 **processor** and has less than 8 megabytes of memory then Windows 3.11 should be the only choice. If your machine has a Pentium processor or equivalent, at least 16 megabytes of memory and a reasonably sized hard drive, then Windows 95/98 will be a better option.

TYPES OF PRINTERS THAT ARE AVAILABLE

At some point you will want to print your work and obviously you are going to need a **printer**. There are various types available – Figure 1 shows three of the most popular choices. The first resembles a dot matrix, the middle one an inkjet and the last one a laser.

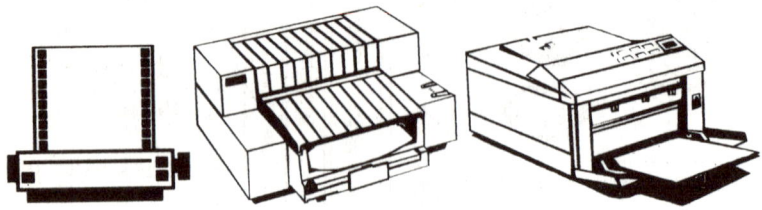

Fig. 1. Samples of printers.

Dot matrix printers are often cheap to buy but tend to be slow and very noisy. **Inkjet** printers are much quieter and give better print quality. Both dot matrix and inkjets are available in mono or colour. **Laser** printers give the best quality printing although the colour laser will be out of most people's price range.

Buying and Setting Up the Computer

PUTTING IT TOGETHER

When you arrive home with your new purchase, connecting all the parts together may at first sight seem a little daunting. You will have a lot of cables but the majority will only fit in one place, so don't worry too much. Refer to Figure 2 to help you.

Locating your computer

When deciding where to position your computer, try to avoid certain areas such as:

- too near a radiator where it may get overheated
- with a window behind you – you may get annoying reflections
- where it will get dusty, eg the floor
- near magnets or radiation-omitting devices as this could damage disks
- anywhere that air will not be able to circulate around the back of the computer.

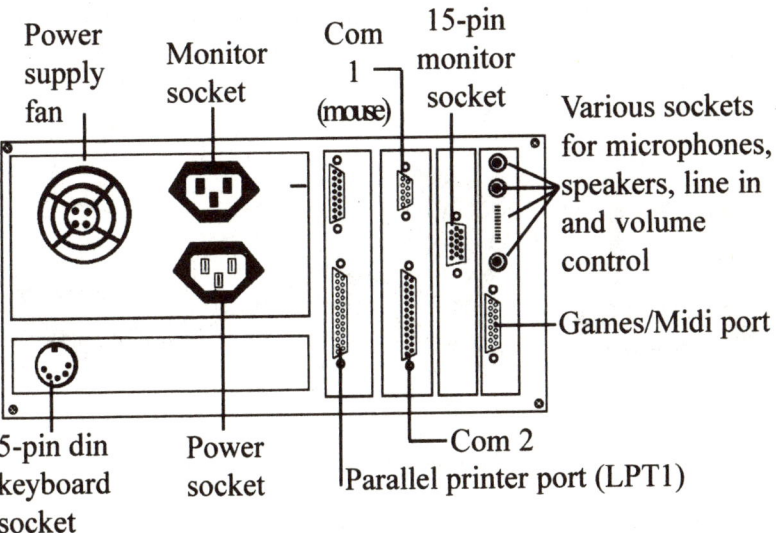

Fig. 2. Rear view of a system unit.

Mouse and keyboard sockets
One minor point to watch out for is the **mouse** and **keyboard** sockets. The most common are shown in the diagram. The other type you may well come across is the PS2 socket, this is similar to the 5-pin din socket but smaller. If you have a PS2 mouse *and* a PS2 keyboard, be sure to put them in their correct sockets. It won't hurt the computer if you fit them the wrong way round, but the system will not start up!

TURNING IT ON

Once you are sure everything is connected correctly you are ready to turn on your computer – **boot up** as it is known. The vast majority of new computers come with the necessary software already installed so it should be ready for you to get started.

Most computers have at least two buttons on the front of the box. One will be for the power, the other will be for re-starting the machine without having to turn the power off. This second button is the **reset** switch.

Monitors that have their power lead direct to the computer are powered from the computer itself. This means that the monitor automatically switches on and off at the same time as you power your computer – providing the on-off button on the monitor itself is left in the on position. Monitors that have a separate power lead need to be turned on and off separately.

Once you've pressed that switch
When a computer is switched on, it runs some self-tests and reads the set-up information from what is called the bios chip – this stands for basic input/output system. Make sure there are no **disks** in the **floppy drive** because this will halt the start up process. If anything is wrong at this stage it will show an error on the monitor screen – contact the helpline! Providing all is well, the computer then initialises its operating system. A message on the screen will state 'Starting MS-DOS' or 'Starting Windows 95/98'. When it has finished the boot-up process, your screen will display one of the following:

- A black screen with a C:\>. You are in the DOS operating system. Refer to the next chapter.

- The Windows 95/98 operating system. Refer to Chapter 4.

- The Program Manager. You are in Windows 3.11. Refer to Chapters 4 and 5.
- If you have anything different from the above three representations, your computer may have what is called a front-end menu system. You will need to refer to your manual for operating instructions.

CASE STUDIES

Mark and Lucy buy a computer
Mark's firm has recently been fully computerised and during the changeover he became convinced that he would be dealing more and more with computers as part of his job. Having discussed the matter, Mark and Lucy decide to buy a new computer system. Before visiting their local computer store they sit down and make a list of the main uses their system will be put to.

- Lucy intends to start an Open University degree and would like to be able to prepare her work, save it and make printouts for study.
- Mark wants to be able to do some of his work at home instead of staying late at the office. Much of his work could be done at home and then taken in to the computers at work once or twice a week.
- Lee is learning to use computers at school and it will be of benefit to him to be able to practise at home.
- Beverly is starting her exam courses at school and they hope her interest in studying can be maintained by having a computer at home.

They decide to buy a mid-range machine that will suit the whole family. They purchase a Pentium 300mz **multimedia** machine with 64 **meg ram**, and a colour inkjet printer. The system comes pre-installed with Windows 98.

Eric and Jean get involved too
Eric, bored with retirement after only three months, has been fascinated by all the talk about computers and decides he wants to get involved. He contacts a friend at his old firm and asks their advice. His friend tells him that they have an older Pentium 133mz computer sitting around doing nothing and asks him if he would

like it on permanent loan to mess about with. The system has 16 meg of ram and has DOS 6.22 and Windows 3.11 installed along with Microsoft Works and a **desktop publisher**. Eric readily accepts the offer and looks forward to collecting it the following day.

PRACTICAL EXERCISE

From the questions asked at the beginning of this chapter, write down what you require a computer for. With the help of the section at the back of this book on Suggested System Requirements, work out what sort of computer you feel you will need to purchase. Go to your local computer store and explain to the salesperson what you feel you would use a computer for and ask for a suggested specification. How close is their verdict to your own?

3
Looking Briefly at DOS

WHAT IS DOS?

No computer book would be complete without at least some reference to DOS. In this chapter we will look at its importance when working with a personal computer. These days most people will find themselves using one version or another of Windows and may not come into direct contact with DOS – but it is still there working in the background. DOS stands for **disc operating system** and comprises a list of commands and instructions used to control the computer.

Before the **graphic user interface** (**GUI**, pronounced goo-ee) was designed, of which Windows is now the most common, you had to learn a fair bit about DOS to use your computer at all. DOS is not very user-friendly and, due to its technical nature and precise syntax requirements, tended to put people off computers pretty effectively. Although you may not need to use it much yourself, the programs you use need it to provide what is known as 'downward compatibility'. This means that as the operating system developed from DOS to Windows, then to Windows 95 and 98, older programs would still work. This saves you having to buy new programs whenever the computer industry has another bright idea!

UNDERSTANDING THE IMPORTANCE OF DOS

DOS not only controls the disks on your computer but it also has to communicate with various other bits and bobs in order that the whole system can work efficiently. When you first start your computer, it loads a file called command.com into the memory. This contains a predefined command set that enables the system to operate. Whatever you do don't delete it, because without it the computer won't work, it will just stare at you and whine 'cannot find command.com'. The only solution to this error is to reload the operating system.

24   Managing Your First Computer

Once DOS has finished setting up the computer it sits and waits for you to give it something to do. During this stage all you will see is a blank screen with the prompt in the top left-hand corner and a flashing cursor looking like this: C:_. When entering any command or instruction you have to press the **enter** key to tell DOS to go off and do something. DOS is not case sensitive, which means that it doesn't care if you use capital letters or small or even a mixture of the two.

Four useful DOS commands
The following commands can be typed at the C:\ prompt and will invoke a reaction when the enter key is pressed.

Time
At some time or another you may have to reset the clock on your computer. In normal circumstances a small battery inside the computer powers a little chip which stores the right time even when the system is turned off. If this battery goes flat, or when the clocks go forward or back, you can reset the time in DOS as follows:

- At the command prompt type the word **time** and press the enter key.

- Type in the new time in the format shown on the screen, eg 10:20:30.1 (hrs. mins. secs.).

- Press the enter key again and hey presto! Job done.

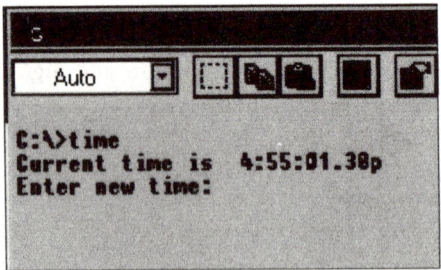

Fig. 3. Sample DOS screen displaying the time.

Why not give it a try now? You can't damage anything. If you are running Windows, you first need to get to the DOS prompt by either shutting down Windows 3.11 or selecting the MSDOS prompt from the start programs menu in Windows 95/98. Your screen will resemble Figure 3.

Looking Briefly at DOS

Date
To alter the date shown by the system just follow the steps above but type the word **date** instead of time.

CD (short for change directory)
This command changes the current working **directory**. Let's say you are in the **root** and you want to change to the DOS directory to find a command. The root of any drive is called '\' known as a **backslash**. You would enter the command **cd dos** – note that after the command **cd** there is a space, this is always the case when entering any command.

To see the files that are in the DOS directory, type **dir** and you will see the list on your screen. To return to the root directory type **CD** – don't forget the space, and to press the enter key afterwards.

Format
Use this command with great care because it is used to destroy all the information held on a disk, including all programs and DOS itself. Only use this on your hard drive if this is what you intend to do. Do ensure that you have the original operating system setup disks available to get your computer running again before you type the command **format C:!**

Its normal use is in preparing new floppy disks to accept data, or for removing all data from a floppy disk prior to reusing it. See the practical exercise at the end of the chapter for using this command.

Disks
There are two types of disk that you may come across – **double density**, which holds 720k of information and **high density**, which holds double that – 1.44meg. If it doesn't say which it is on the label you can tell by looking at the rear edge of the disk. Double density disks have only one hole with a switch on the back that enables you to write-protect it. High-density disks have two holes, with the switch on only one. Any computer that is less than five years old will be able to work with 1.44 disks. The 720K disks are not worth buying now.

What is write-protection?
If the hole is in the closed position, ie you cannot see through it, the disk is *not* write-protected. Anything can be written to or read from the disk. If the hole is in the open position, the disk is write-protected: you can only read from this disk and not write to it, so

the data already on the disk is protected and cannot be overwritten.

LOOKING AT TWO SYSTEM FILES

The **autoexec.bat** and **config.sys** – found in the root directory – are not technically required for the computer to work, but it may behave a little strangely if they are not there. These files contain information that enables the computer to be personalised and will tell the system such things as what type of screen you have, what mouse you are using and what language you are speaking. They will also load programs called drivers that operate things like **sound cards**, **scanners** and CD-ROM drives without which these devices will not work.

It is a good idea to make a copy of these files on a floppy disk just in case they ever get deleted or damaged by accident. If ever your computer acts strangely when you turn it on the likelihood is that one of these files has been corrupted.

CASE STUDY

Eric customises his boot-up procedure

Eric's grandson likes to play on his computer when he and Jean are minding him. As Lee's computer has Windows 98 he has difficulty when Grandad's starts up in DOS. Eric decides to make a little alteration so that Windows is automatically started when the computer boots up. To do this, at the DOS command prompt he types **edit autoexec.bat**. This opens the DOS editor program and loads in a copy of his autoexec.bat file ready for changing. He moves the cursor to the bottom of the text and adds the following new line – **win** – which is the command that starts Windows running. He then saves the file and returns to the DOS prompt. In future when he starts the computer it will automatically start Windows running and Lee will be happy.

PRACTICAL EXERCISE

Format a high-density floppy disk in DOS using the following steps.

1. Ensure the disk is not write-protected and insert it into the floppy disk drive.

2. At the command prompt type **format a:**.

Looking Briefly at DOS

3. The computer gives you a warning that all data will be lost and will ask you if you still wish to go ahead. Press the **y** key for yes and press **enter**.

4. The computer will then remind you to insert a disk in the drive A and press any key when ready. Assuming the disk is in the drive pressing any key on your keyboard starts the formatting process.

5. The screen will indicate the percentage progress and on completion will ask if you wish to enter a **volume label**. Unless you have a strong sentimental reason for giving your disks their own names just press the enter key to ignore this message.

6. The formatting process is now complete and the next screen will give you information about the formatted structure.

A word of warning at this point
If the screen reports any bad sectors on the disk, throw it away. They are fairly cheap these days and bad sectors are a sign that it is becoming unreliable. Valuable data could be lost if you use it.

Formatting the less popular double density disk is similar to the above but you will have to tell DOS that it is not a high-density disk or it will report an error. To do this, at stage two above instead of **format a:** type **format a: /f: 720**.

SUMMARY

The pros of DOS
- DOS, in one form or another, is necessary for all PCs to operate at the present time.
- Being familiar with DOS gives you greater control of your machine.
- A good working knowledge of DOS will help pinpoint problems.

The cons of DOS
- DOS is boring if you're not computer minded.
- DOS requires commands to be entered very precisely.
- Trying to use DOS if you're not familiar with it can be risky.
- DOS can be very difficult to get the hang of.
- There are no pretty pictures in DOS.

4
Exploring Windows 95/98

Windows 98 is not a new operating system, it is merely an update to Windows 95 and will work in exactly the same way. Where enhancements or minor changes do exist, these will be indicated in the text.

USING A MOUSE

Windows 95/98 is a GUI (graphic user interface) and gives the user the ability to perform many key functions using a *mouse*. The screen is known as your **desktop**. On your screen will be a small pointed arrowhead, this is the **cursor**. If you move your mouse around, the arrowhead will move with it. There are various ways in which a mouse is used.

Click or single click
This means pressing the left button on your mouse once and releasing it. First place the point of the arrowhead at the item you wish to select, then press down and release the left mouse button.

Right click
As above, but using the right mouse button. You can right click on just about anything in Windows 95/98, which normally produces a further menu for making selections using a left click.

Double click
Some actions require just a single click of the mouse. Others, such as starting a program running from an icon, require a double click. This means two rapid clicks of the same button in succession. It can take a bit of getting used to, but persevere and you will soon have the hang of it. Windows 98 will allow you to single click in place of double click by tagging the **click saver** selection in Settings/Control Panel/Mouse.

Exploring Windows 95/98

Highlight
Selecting or highlighting an item tells the computer what you wish to work with. Pointing the mouse cursor at an item and clicking with the left button can highlight some things, such as icons. However, sometimes, in a word processor for example, the arrowhead will change into an I-bar shape. Selecting is carried out by placing the I-bar at beginning of your text, holding down the mouse button and dragging it over the required selection.

Changing the click
If you are left-handed, you can reverse the clicking action on your mouse to make it more comfortable for you. This can be changed in the mouse section of the **control panel**, which will be explained later.

WHERE DO I BEGIN?

At the bottom of the screen is a long bar, this is called the **task bar**. At one end is the word **Start**. This is where you begin looking at the menus. At the other end is displayed the time. When you use a program, the task bar will display a button with the name of your program on it. If you have more than one program open at a time, you can easily switch between them by clicking the appropriate task bar button with your mouse. Doing this will bring your selected program into view, leaving other open programs tucked behind. With Windows 98, click on this button to shrink the program you're working in – called minimising. This allows you quick access to your desktop icons. Figure 4 shows a task bar with two programs running.

Fig. 4. Task bar with two programs open.

Keeping track of the time
Double clicking on the time display displays the clock properties for you to alter if you wish. Just holding your mouse arrowhead over the time for a second or two will produce the date. Right clicking on the task bar itself takes you to the properties section of the menu system.

Beginning at the start

Click on the start button to display the first fly-out **menu**. Some of the menu descriptions such as **Programs** and **Settings** will have further menus. These will be indicated with small black arrows at the side. Holding your mouse arrowhead over the menu description produces the sub-menu – you do not have to click it. The contents of the menu will vary according to what is installed on the computer. Windows 98 positions some items in a slightly different place to Windows 95, along with a couple of additions such as **Favorites** and the **Log Off** command that can be used in conjunction with different users setting their desktops to individual tastes.

To start a program that is already installed on your machine, search through these menus until you find the appropriate program, then point and click. Figure 5 shows how to start the **Paint** program. After clicking on Start, point to Programs, then to Accessories, move the arrowhead down to the word Paint, and click – the program opens and a program button will be displayed on your task bar.

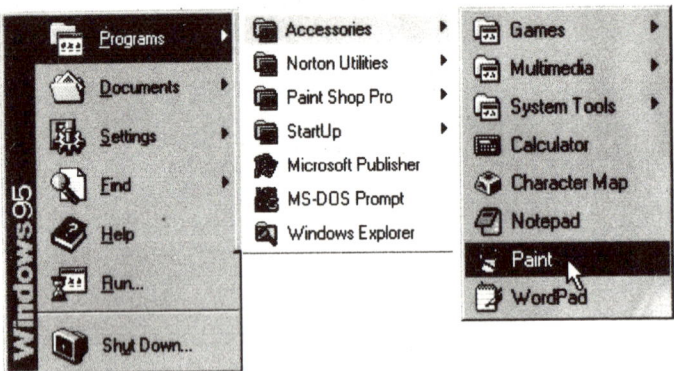

Fig. 5. Fly-out menu system.

CHARACTERISTICS OF THE WINDOWS

When a program is open, it will run inside a window as seen in Figure 6. Every window has the same characteristics and tools enabling you to resize, close and move them around as you wish. We will look at these characteristics with the Paint program window that should still be displayed from the previous section.

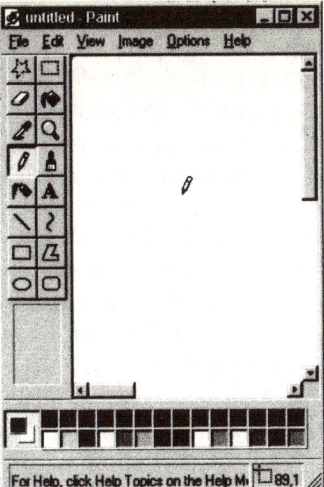

Fig. 6. A window.

At the very top of the window is a shaded area that has the name of the program on it. This is called the **title bar**. At the moment it will be showing **untitled – Paint** because you have not yet given it a name. Underneath the title bar is a row of words – these are **menu options**. These menu options appear on all programs. Each one, when clicked on with the mouse, produce a **drop-down** list of available commands that allows you to perform tasks such as saving your work, printing or altering it.

To the right of the title bar are three small icons that look like buttons.

- The first one resembles a small line or a minus sign, this is the **minimise** button. When you click on this, the program stays open but is minimised. The window disappears but can be restored from the task bar.

- The second one resembles a box, this is the **maximise** button. When you click on this the program will be displayed at the window's largest size. The icon then changes to two smaller boxes; clicking on this restores it to its previous size.

- The third one resembles a cross, this is the **close** button. This closes down a window that you have finished working with. If you have not saved your work, you will be prompted to do so before the window closes.

If the size of your window is smaller than the size of your screen, you can move the window around by placing your mouse arrowhead onto the title bar, holding down the left mouse button and dragging it to a new position.

Scrolling around

To understand the use of the **scroll bars** properly, you can do a little practical work. Enlarge the size of the window a little by placing your mouse pointer at the bottom right-hand corner of the window. When you see the arrowhead change to a double head, press down the left mouse button and hold. Drag the window to a larger size. Now draw something in the working area of the Paint program as follows:

1. With your mouse, select the rectangle from the tool bar on the left.

2. Move to the working area. Your mouse arrowhead will have changed to a cross.

3. Position the cross at the top left-hand corner of the working area and hold down the left mouse button. Drag the box shape to the bottom right-hand corner and release the mouse.

4. Select the 'fill with colour' icon, which looks like a tin of paint being spilt.

5. Select a colour from the palette at the bottom of the window.

6. Place your mouse inside the rectangle and click – it will fill with colour.

Scroll bars appear when the contents of a window are larger than the window itself. The scroll bar on the right allows you to move up and down your document, the one at the bottom allows you to move left and right. If you do not have any scroll bars showing at present, then reduce the size of the window again and they will appear. Now, if you click and hold down your mouse button on the slider control of the right-hand scroll bar and move it up and down, you will see your rectangle moving. Do the same with the bottom scroll bar.

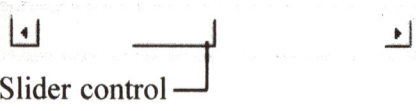

Fig. 7. A scroll bar.

Exploring Windows 95/98

As Figure 7 shows, scroll bars can be used in three ways:

- click and hold on the slider control dragging it along
- clicking outside the slider control area moves the view instantly
- using the arrows at either end of the bar moves the view in small stages.

Windows within windows

Some programs have windows within windows. A word processing program is a typical example. You will have the program window itself, which will have the usual title bar naming the program, menu selections, minimise, maximise and close buttons. Inside this will be your **document** window – this will have its own title bar but contain the name of your document. It too will have min/max and close buttons but will not have the menu selections. You use the menu selections from the main window. When you wish to maximise, minimise or close a window be sure to select the correct set of buttons.

PERSONALISING THE DESKTOP

You can change the way your desktop looks and acts using **desktop display properties**. To open this, right click on a blank area of the initial screen of Windows 95 or 98 and then click on the **properties** selection in the menu that appears. In this you can:

- paste **wallpapers** onto our desktop
- set up **screen savers**
- change the **background colour** of your desktop
- change the appearance of your **title bars** and **tool bars**
- change the settings of the **fonts** and **colours** that are displayed.

The dialogue box displayed gives four choices: **Background**, **Screen Saver**, **Appearance** and **Settings**. This is where you make your choices – see Figure 8. There is a mock monitor screen that will give you a sample of your choice when you select **Apply** at the bottom of the box.

Designing the decor

Select the **Background** tab at the top of the box. On the left you have a selection of patterns, on the right a selection of wallpapers. The only difference between the two is that patterns display a maximum

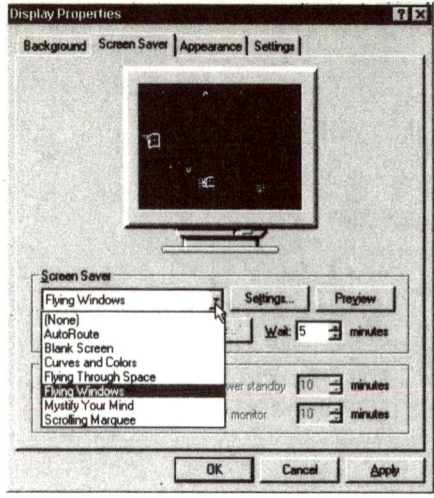

Fig. 8. Screen saver dialogue box.

of two colours, wallpapers display more. It is best to select one or the other, ie if you select a wallpaper, have the pattern setting at **None** and vice versa.

Click on each pattern in turn and see the effect it gives you on the mock monitor. With the wallpapers, ensure you have the display setting on **Tile** to ensure that the whole screen is covered.

Windows 98 differences
The display is slightly different on the **Background** tab, listing all the wallpapers, and more of them, in one column. The **Pattern** feature can still be accessed by clicking the pattern button. There are further options for dressing your desktop that can be found in the Control Panel by clicking on **Desktop Themes**. With this you can place pictures of animals, trees, space objects plus more onto your desktop.

Saving the screen
A screen saver is a moving picture that displays on your screen when you are not using it. The idea is to stop an image burning into the screen of your monitor if it is left on for a long time without use. There are a few basic screen savers built into Windows 95, with some more interesting ones in Windows 98, especially if a Desktop Theme

Exploring Windows 95/98   35

has been chosen. You can find these in the display properties box by clicking on the **Screen Saver** tab at the top.

In Figure 8 the screen saver **Flying Windows** has been selected. Using the **Settings** button you can configure the speed that the windows fly at, and the amount of windows there are. In the **Wait** box a time delay can be entered to tell the computer when to activate the saver. Ten minutes is an appropriate delay – this means that if you have not used your keyboard or mouse for a period of ten minutes, the screen saver will become active. You can see a sample of the screen saver by clicking on **Preview**. Once you have settled on a choice, remember to click on **Apply** or **OK** before closing the window.

Colouring your backgrounds and title bars

Click on the **Appearance** tab of the dialogue box and you have the opportunity to completely change your colour scheme. Each of the three description boxes – **Scheme**, **Item** and **Font** – allow you to change the relevant display. At the side of each box can be found individual settings for size and colour. Once again, you will be able to see the effects on the mock monitor. Don't forget to click **Apply** when you have settled on a scheme.

THE ICONS ON YOUR SCREEN

When you start up your computer you will see a number of icons on your desktop. These are the small graphics or pictures. You will have at least two or more of the following as shown in Figure 9.

Recycle Bin   My Computer   Network   Inbox   Set Up The   My Briefcase
                            Neighborhood   Microsoft
                                                     Network

Fig. 9. Sample icons on a desktop.

- **The Recycle Bin**. This is an important trashcan that will be explained soon.
- **My Computer**. This enables you to view all the files on your computer.
- **Network Neighbourhood**. This is used when two or more computers are linked together. The help files will explain about using this if it applies to you.

- **Inbox**. This is used for fax and e-mail messaging – again see the help files.

- **Set up the Microsoft Network**. An **Internet Service Provider**. Refer to Chapter 14 for more information on this.

- **My Briefcase**. For keeping files in order when using more than one computer for the same work, such as a laptop and a PC. Refer to the manual or help files for this too.

Keeping your environment friendly with the recycle bin

Whenever you delete anything from your hard drive, Windows 95/98 automatically sends it to the recycle bin. This does not happen when you delete files from another drive such as the floppy disk – so please do remember that, and be careful.

While deleted files are stored in the recycle bin, they are retrievable. This may be very handy to you one day when you suddenly realise you have deleted something by mistake. Simply double click on the recycle bin icon, right click on the file that was deleted and select **restore** from the menu.

Using it to its full advantage
The recycle bin is a safeguard not found in previous versions of Windows and should be used to its full advantage. When you do delete files, always leave them stored in the recycle bin until you have used your computer for a while – especially the program from which you have deleted the files. If you find, when subsequently using your computer, that things seem to be drastically wrong, it may turn out that you had accidentally deleted an important system or program file. If it is still stored in the recycle bin, it can be restored without too much effort. Once you have used your computer without failure, you know it is safe to empty the recycle bin, which can be done by choosing this option from the file menu.

Exploring the My Computer icon

Double clicking on this icon produces a window that shows available **drives** and gives an opportunity to configure other parts of your computer using the control panel and the printer's folder. Each one of these icons can be double clicked to see what is 'inside' them. By using the My Computer icon, it is easy to fill your desktop with windows, becoming confused as to exactly what you are looking at.

In Windows 95/98 there is always more than one way of doing the same thing and My Computer icon is no exception. The alternative, and much simpler way, to view your various drives is with the **Windows Explorer** which is explained in detail in Chapter 8. The control panel and printers areas can be easily accessed from the start menu by choosing **Settings**. You will no doubt at some time experiment with both systems and find out which is best for you.

WINDOWS 95/98 ACCESSORIES

Windows comes with a few very basic, but nevertheless interesting little programs. The paint program that was used earlier to explain the characteristics of the windows is one of them.

Other programs

Games
Solitaire, Hearts and Minesweeper are popular and valuable. They are a fun way to become proficient at using the mouse. Find them through the fly-out menus at Start/Programs/Accessories/Games.

Calculator
Use this as you would a normal calculator but using either your mouse or the keyboard to enter the details. There are two calculators for you to use, a scientific or a normal one. If you need to use a calculator whilst working at your computer, why not have them open and minimised on the task bar for instant use.

WordPad
This is a very basic word processor. If you do not have a separate word processor installed on your machine, you can use this one. See Chapter 10 for details on the functions available and how to use them.

Notepad
Think of this as a jotting pad for brief notes.

Multimedia
This gives you the ability to play your music CDs in the CD-ROM while using other programs, and to record sounds and adjust volumes.

System tools
These allow you to keep your computer healthy by giving it a service every now and again. See Chapter 7 for more details on using these.

Using Help as another accessory

The help files are very useful in all programs. The Windows 95/98 Help is of course just designed for looking at questions and problems with Windows itself. If you need help with a particular program, start up that program and initiate help from there.

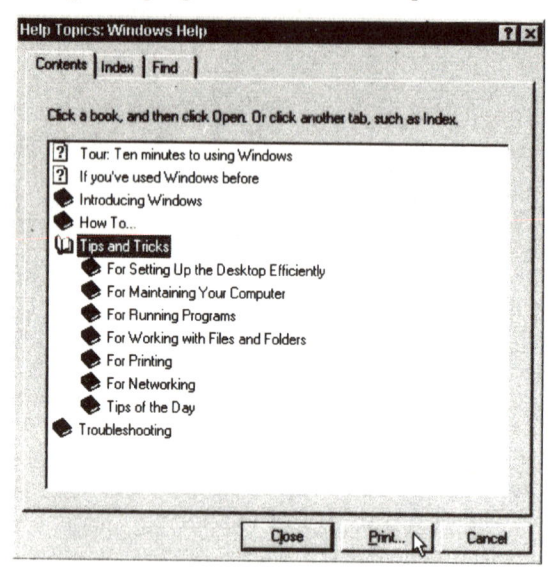

Fig. 10. A help window.

Select Help from the Start menu. A dialogue box appears to assist you in locating your topic, as shown in Figure 10. The **Contents** tab has overall topics that are useful to work through when you have some spare time. Each of the displayed topics has a further, more in-depth menu when they are double clicked as shown in the diagram. The **Index** tab allows you to enter a particular word that then leads you to more widespread information. One disadvantage with the index choice is that you need to have an idea what the subject is named in order to begin looking for it.

Topics can be printed out and read at your leisure by clicking on the print command either at the bottom of the dialogue box, or from the **Options** menu. Spend time learning to use the help files as they are very comprehensive and once you know how they work will be of continuing benefit.

Shutting down

It is important to turn off your computer the correct way when you have finished using it. This is because the system files continually update themselves ready for the next time you use the computer. If you do not switch off correctly, these files may not get updated properly. Most problems new users come across are as a direct result of not turning the computer off correctly.

Windows makes it easy for you to accomplish this by giving you a **Shut Down** command in the Start menu. After selecting this, you are given a list of choices as shown in Figure 11. Select the appropriate button and click on Yes (or No if you have made a mistake) and your computer will begin the correct shut down mode. If you

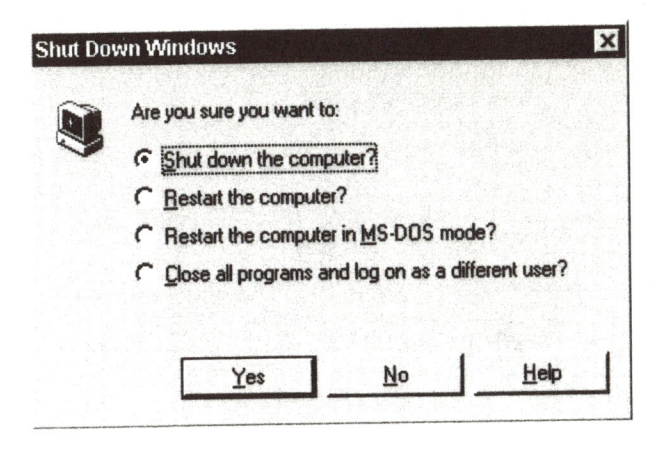

Fig. 11. The shut down dialogue box.

selected to turn it off for the day, a message will be displayed after a few seconds telling you that it is now safe to turn off your computer.

Restarting in DOS mode
If you selected to restart in DOS mode, the Windows program shuts down correctly. However, in order to keep your computer working, it renames some of the Windows system files so that DOS can understand where things are. To see how to find your way around DOS refer to Chapter 3. When you have finished using the DOS mode, type **Exit** at the C:\ prompt. This allows Windows to restart, renaming the files as it does so, and you can then shut down for the day as described in the previous section. Always return to Windows to shut down – never just turn off your computer in DOS mode.

CASE STUDY

Mark's conversion to Windows 95

Although Mark is familiar with using computers at work, his firm still uses Windows 3.11 so he is unsure of Windows 95. In order to find his way around he spends a couple of hours just experimenting. He makes liberal use of the help files when he comes across things he isn't sure of and he completes the **Windows 95 Tour**.

At the end of the session he has found, much to his relief, that the skills learned at work can still be applied to his own computer. He finds that, although very different in appearance, the techniques translate easily from one system to the other. He will be able to apply all these skills confidently in Windows 98 as well.

PRACTICAL EXERCISE

Set up a Screen Saver:

1. Right click in an empty space on the desktop to display the menu, left click on selection called **Properties**.

2. Select the screen saver tab by clicking on it.

3. Click on the arrow next to the screen saver selection box and scroll down until you find **Scrolling Marque**, click on this to select it.

4. Click on the **Settings** tab, select **Random** placement and turn the speed up to **Fast** by dragging the button along the bar.

5. Change the **Background Colour** to green.

6. Highlight the text bar with your mouse – type in a message you wish to display.

7. Click on **Format text** and choose a style of writing, along with a large font size, click OK.

8. Click the OK button again in this box.

9. Change the **Wait** time to 10 minutes – this is when the screen saver will become active.

10. Click on **Preview** to see what your choices will look like.

11. Finally, press any key on the keyboard, or click the mouse button to halt the preview and click OK. Your saver is now operational.

5
Exploring Windows 3.11

Windows versions prior to Windows 95 need DOS installed in order to run. To start Windows, type **Win** at the DOS prompt. The program uses a graphic user interface (GUI), in which the mouse, rather than the keyboard, is used to give instructions to the computer. The mouse is operated in a similar fashion to Windows 95 but the right button is not used.

Both Windows versions are very similar in operation – Windows 95 is an updated version of 3.11, with a new look start-up screen and fly-out menu system instead of Program Manager. In order to avoid repetition, this chapter will deal with those procedures that differ substantially from Windows 95. Procedures common to both versions, and already dealt with in Chapter 4 include:

- use of the mouse
- characters of the windows
- scroll bars
- personalising the desktop.

Although some of the dialogue boxes may be slightly different in appearance, the actual commands will be the same.

WHERE DO I BEGIN?

Windows 3.11 starts with the **program manager**. This is itself a large window with other windows inside. It is from the program manager that you access all other programs by selecting the icons contained in the various windows.

Instead of using a menu system, programs store their start-up icons in separate windows known as **groups**. These windows can be shrunk to icon size, then accessed again by double clicking on them. In Figure 12 there are five windows shrunk to icon size; this is known as its minimised state. The **Main** window has been opened to reveal the icons inside it.

As programs are launched by double clicking on their icons it's an important technique to master. If you haven't got the hang of double clicking yet, you can select the icon so that it is highlighted, then click on the **File** menu just underneath the title bar and select **Run**.

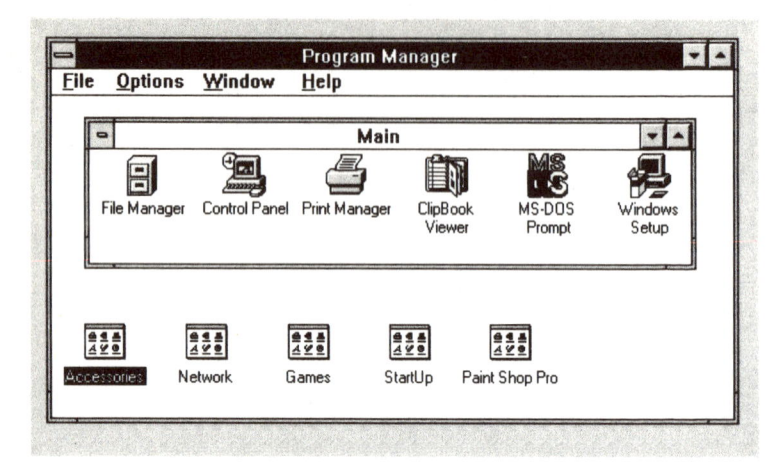

Fig. 12. Program manager in Windows 3.11.

CHARACTERISTICS OF THE WINDOWS

Windows can be moved around and altered in size as described in the previous chapter, but one major difference with Windows 3.11 is that you do not have a task bar. This does not stop you having more than one window open at a time, though. You can have as many open as you wish, but they will be stacked one in front of the other, preventing you from seeing them all. As soon as you click on a window, it becomes active and will appear at the front. 'Don't you have to be able to see it first?' you may say. Yes, and this can be done in any of the following ways:

- **Alt** and **Tab**. By holding your thumb down on the alt key on your keyboard, then pressing the tab key as shown in Figure 13, you can flick through all the open windows. When the window you wish to view is selected, lift your finger and thumb off the keys.

- **Tile**. You can tile all of the open windows across your desktop by clicking on the command in the Window menu just below the title bar.

Exploring Windows 3.11

- **Cascade**. The windows can be displayed in a cascaded view by selecting this command from the Window menu as above.

Fig. 13. Pressing the alt and tab keys.

In Windows 3.11 the maximise/minimise and close buttons are displayed differently from Windows 95. The close button is on the left-hand top corner of the window and looks like a small dash. The minimise button is the down arrow on the right-hand top corner, the maximise button is the up arrow next to it. These can be seen in Figure 12.

PERSONALISING THE DESKTOP

The desktop can be given a personal touch by using the control panel icon found in the main window. Double clicking on the desktop icon produces the dialogue box to change your wallpapers and screen savers, plus a few extras such as the sizes of the borders around your windows and how close the icons are placed together. You do not have the mock monitor to preview your choices, but you can have a look at the screen saver by clicking on **Test**.

The **Colours** icon allows you to alter the colour scheme of your desktop. With this you can change the background or the colours of the title bars.

Saving your screen appearance

Windows 3.11 has a **Save Settings** feature. Once you have designed your desktop to your liking you can 'save' it to ensure it will always appear that way.

1. Go to the **Options** menu and ensure **Save Settings on Exit** is

ticked. This will tell the program that the way you have set up your display is how you want it to always appear.

2. **Exit from Windows**. Closing the Windows program down ensures that your settings will be entered in the set-up files.

3. **Restart Windows** and **unmark** the Save Settings on Exit. Your new settings will now be in use. The selection needs to be unmarked to ensure it is not 'overwritten' by accident.

Now, each time you run Windows, its appearance will be the same regardless of what it looked like when you last closed it down.

CREATING NEW WINDOWS AND ICONS

Selecting **New** from the file menu in program manager can create a new window and/or icon. The dialogue box asks which you wish to create as shown in Figure 14.

- **Program Group** is a window
- **Program Item** is an icon.

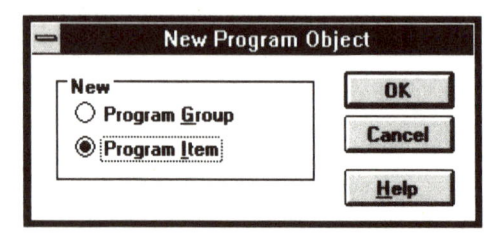

Fig. 14. New program object dialogue box.

Creating a new program group

This is simply a case of typing in the name you wish to call your new window then clicking OK. Windows will do the rest – see Figure 15.

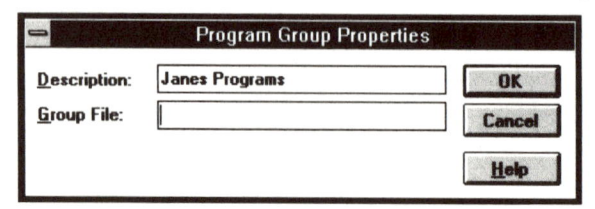

Fig. 15. New program group dialogue box.

Creating a new program item

This is slightly more difficult as you have to give the computer more information, and it has to be correct for it to work properly as shown in Figure 16.

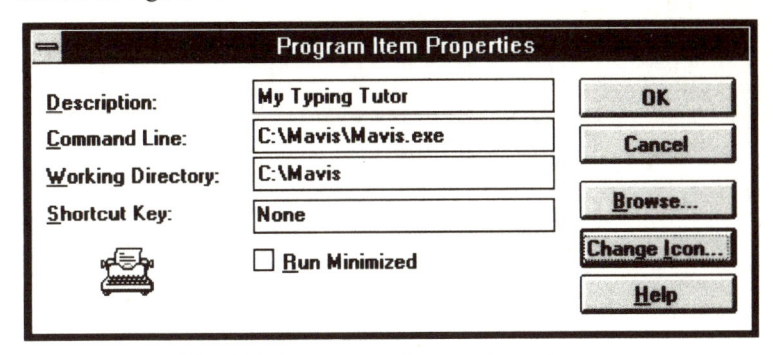

```
┌─────────────────── Program Item Properties ───────────────────┐
  Description:       [My Typing Tutor      ]        [   OK    ]
  Command Line:      [C:\Mavis\Mavis.exe   ]        [ Cancel  ]
  Working Directory: [C:\Mavis             ]
  Shortcut Key:      [None                 ]        [ Browse..]
                     ☐ Run Minimized                [Change Icon..]
                                                    [  Help   ]
```

Fig. 16. New program item dialogue box.

First type in the description you wish to give your icon – this will be its label. In the command line you have to direct the computer to the executable file that starts your program running. You can either type this in if you know it, or the browse button can be used to search for the relevant file. Once found, double clicking on it will complete the command line for you.

Next, enter in the **Working Directory** box the name of the directory where you want any saved files to be stored. If you do not fill this box in then files will be saved in the program's own directory. You can then name a shortcut by pressing the desired key on your keyboard – this means you can either double click on your finished icon to start it, or press the relevant shortcut key. If you wish your icon to have a specific graphical design, click on **Change Icon** and make your choice from those shown. Click on OK when you have finished and try your new icon out.

Moving icons from window to window

Icons can be selected and dragged from one window to another using the mouse pointer. This will not affect the way it works.

Icons, and windows when they are empty of icons, can be removed by highlighting them and pressing the **delete** key on your keyboard. Deleting them does not remove the program from your computer, just the icon. To remove a program, refer to Chapter 9.

WINDOWS 3.11 ACCESSORIES

The icons for these programs are held in the **Accessories** window.

- **Write** is a basic word processor. Refer to Chapter 10 on word processing.
- **Paintbrush** is a drawing program, the same as Paint in Windows 95/98.
- **Calculator** and **Clock** are self-explanatory.
- **Calendar** is a small personal diary program.
- **Cardfile** is a simple record card filing system.

Calendar and cardfile were not taken over into Windows 95/98, probably because they were so very basic. However, each member of the family can have their own separate file with their own set of appointments and record lists.

- Cardfile is a very basic database. It consists of a set of blank cards that are used to store information such as names, addresses and telephone numbers. These can then be printed out.
- Calendar can display times of the day to log important appointments. Events can be set to trigger an alarm display, for example to pop up a message – 'Only two minutes left till Eastenders'.

CASE STUDY

Eric gets to grips with his mouse

Eric has had no previous experience with computers. In DOS he can use the keyboard, with which he is familiar, but he finds it tedious. Windows 3.11 is a totally new experience for him and he finds that using the mouse requires hand-eye co-ordination that he is finding difficult. Following advice from Mark, he acquires this skill by playing with the games that are in Windows. He also enjoys himself and discovers that learning can be fun, even for those who are a little older.

PRACTICAL EXERCISE

Play a game which will get you used to using the mouse.

1. Open the Games window either by double clicking on it, or by single clicking and choosing **Restore** from the menu that appears.

2. Open the **Minesweeper** game by using the above method on its icon.

3. Click on the help menu and have a read about how the game should be played. The help screen shows you a list of options. Click on each one in turn to see their contents.

4. Begin the game by clicking your left mouse cursor on any square. If you are unlucky enough to hit a mine straightaway, the game will be over. Click on the smiley face above the grid to try again.

5. Uncovering a figure tells you how many mines are next to that square. When, through a process of elimination you know where a mine is, click on the right mouse button over the square and a flag will be put on it.

6. Clicking a second time over the square puts a question mark on it, clicking yet again returns it to being blank – but don't forget, this is using the right click on the mouse.

7. There are two digital figures at the top of the window, as you will see in Figure 17. The left one tells you how many mines you have left to find, the right one will be monitoring the time it takes you to find them.

8. When you become familiar with the game, click on the game menu and choose a harder level. Good luck!

Fig. 17. Minesweeper game.

6
Sorting Out Drives, Paths and Trees

Computers are very logical devices – they like to know where everything is and they like to be kept neat and tidy. This is achieved with a filing system composed of **drives**, **paths** and **trees**.

DEFINING DRIVE LETTER NAMES

Disk drives on the computer are given different letters of the alphabet as names. This enables the user to tell the computer where to look for information. The normal convention for naming drives is as follows:

- first floppy drive: A drive
- second floppy drive (if fitted):   B drive
- hard disk: C drive
- CD-ROM (if fitted):   D drive

Some hard drives may have partitions that split the drive into two or more sections. When this is the case the first partition will normally be the C drive and the second part the D drive. Drive letter E would then be assigned to the CD-ROM. Any other drives available, via a network for instance, would be assigned subsequent letters, i.e. F, G, etc.

EXPLAINING THE TREE STRUCTURE

Computers work more efficiently if a good tree structure is developed. The tree is a representation of how files are stored on computer disks. This can be the hard disk, a floppy disk or a CD-ROM. The tree, as shown in Figure 18, has a root and branches that can be compared to an office filing cabinet. The root is the cabinet for storing all the information. The branches contain the **Directories** (Windows 3.11) or **Folders** (Windows 95/98) – these can be compared with the drawers of the filing cabinet. Inside the drawers

Sorting Out Drives, Paths and Trees

are the files.

In a filing cabinet drawer you have cardboard files that hold all the loose-leaf papers relevant to that file: in the computer's tree you can have **sub-directories** of directories, or folders leading off other folders. In an ideal office, paperwork is always stored in its relevant place neatly in the cabinet. In an ideal computer set-up there is a well-structured tree with relevant files placed in ideally positioned folders not all thrown in the root.

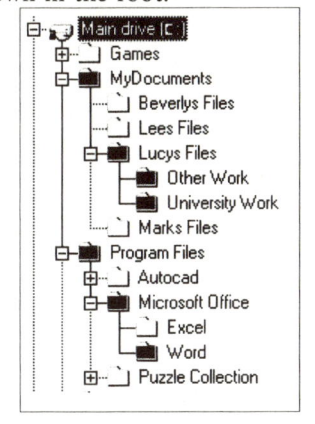

```
├─ Main drive (C:)
│  ├─ Games
│  ├─ MyDocuments
│  │  ├─ Beverlys Files
│  │  ├─ Lees Files
│  │  ├─ Lucys Files
│  │  │  ├─ Other Work
│  │  │  └─ University Work
│  │  └─ Marks Files
│  ├─ Program Files
│  │  ├─ Autocad
│  │  └─ Microsoft Office
│  │     ├─ Excel
│  │     └─ Word
│  └─ Puzzle Collection
```

Fig. 18. A tree structure.

NAMING DIRECTORIES/FOLDERS AND FILES

All information is stored on a computer in **files**. A program consists of one or more files and will normally occupy its own folder within the tree. Folders and files can be given any name but for a few exceptions, although it is good practice to use a close description relevant to the contents. File names normally have what is called an **extension** of three characters after a dot. For example, if you create a file and save it with the name of English Essay, the program will add its own relative extension. If this happens to be a word processor that uses the extension **.doc** your filename will now be English Essay.doc – although you may not see this extension.

Which characters cannot be used in filenames?
1. **Full stops**. Because the computer will get confused with its extension.
2. **?** or *****. Because these are used by the computer for other functions known as wildcards.

3. :. Because this is used after a letter to denote a drive name.

4. / \ | | < > + = or ,. These all have specific meanings to the computer.

In DOS and Windows versions prior to Windows 95 you are limited to eight characters for a directory or file name and you cannot use spaces. If you attempt to name a file using more than eight characters, you may be given the 'incorrect filename' error, or the program will only accept the first eight characters. Bear this in mind if you are going to give somebody else a file. If they are using Windows 3.11 and you name a file using more than eight characters in Windows 95/98, their system may not be able to recognise it.

Finding the right folder

The rule of giving folders and files names to indicate their content is common practice with manufacturers of programs. This means that if you wish to move or delete a program that has previously been installed on your computer, it should be easy to find. In Windows 95/98, folders are often named with the full name of the program, although they may be tucked away in the **Program Files** folder. In Windows 3.11 and with DOS programs, the names will be shortened to a maximum of eight characters. The **Microsoft Office** program, for example, is installed into the **Program Files** folder. This creates a new folder with the name Microsoft Office. Each program within Office such as Word, will then be installed in a sub-folder with the relevant name as seen in Figure 18.

WORKING WITH THE PATH COMMAND

The route you take to get to a file is called its path. A path always starts at the root, ie **C:**. The C: indicates which drive the file is located on, the \, or **backslash** as it is known, indicates that you are starting at the root. You then follow the path till you reach the file required, naming each directory or folder you need to pass through. Think of it as a map giving the computer directions to your file.

Figure 18 shows a sample tree. The English Essay file has been stored in the University Work folder. It was written in Microsoft Word and has the .doc extension. The computer path command to the file is as follows:

C:\MyDocuments\Lucys Files\University Work\English Essay.doc

CASE STUDY

Lucy organises her family

Lucy has been using the computer to write her letters and assignments to the Open University and other establishments. She notices that Mark's letters, and her children's homework and jottings are also in the same folder, and in fairly large numbers. Fearing for the security of her future work and projects, she decides to create a folder for each member of the family and move the files into their relevant folders. She also creates subfolders for herself to keep her University material separate from her general correspondence.

By tidying up the tree structure of the hard disk, each member of the family will now be able to find their files more quickly and **backups** to floppy will be made much easier. There is also less likelihood of one of the children tampering with her work out of curiosity.

PRACTICAL EXERCISE

In this exercise you can create the new folders for everyone to store their own work. We will do this using the my computer icon. This can be achieved in Windows explorer as well, which is covered in more depth in Chapter 8.

1. Double click on the my computer icon on your desktop. A window will appear, showing you the available disk drives on your computer.

2. Double click on the C:\ drive. You are now in the root directory of your hard drive. You will see the folders and files that are stored on your computer.

3. Click on the file menu at the top of the window, then point and click at **New** and **Folder** respectively. This tells Windows that you want to create a new folder off the root directory.

4. You will see a new yellow folder appear with the label highlighted waiting for you to name.

5. Type in **Our Files** and press the enter key on your keyboard. Your first folder is created.

6. Double click on your new folder. An empty window will appear. Follow the same procedure again from step three to create a folder for yourself.

7. When you've completed that, click in the white area of that window to de-select your folder. Click on file, new and folder again and create ones for your partner and children.

8. Double click on your own folder. Another empty window will appear. Create yourself two more folders called Private and Work.

To save files to these folders, use the **Save As...** command from the program you are using. In the dialogue box, name your file and direct it to save it in C:\OurFiles\???\work etc by double clicking on the root directory, and then each folder in turn until arriving at your own.

7
Understanding Your Disk Drives

Whilst it is operating, a computer uses programs to perform the tasks you require of it. Programs can be very large and need to be stored somewhere so that the computer can find them. Also, when you have done some work you may want to save it so that you can refer to it again later. This is what disk drives are for. They are described as mass storage devices because of the large amounts of information they can hold. There are three main types of disk drives in most computers. Two of these, the floppy and the hard drive work in a similar fashion. The third, the CD-ROM is slightly different.

WORKING WITH FLOPPY DISKS

There is some information about floppy disks in the chapter on DOS earlier in this book. Here is a little more.

So what is the floppy disk drive?

There are two sizes of floppy disk drive, 5.25-inch and 3.5-inch, illustrated in Figure 19. The 5.25-inch is very rare in today's computers and uses a paper-covered disk of thin plastic. This is where the term floppy disk comes from. The more common 3.5-inch drive uses a much more rigid plastic case with a metal protection slide. The disk is inserted into the slot on the front of the computer and locks into place. A small indication light comes on when a disk is being used and there is a button that enables you to eject a disk from the drive. It is often referred to as the **A:\ drive**.

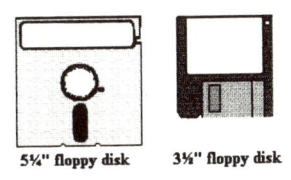

5¼" floppy disk   3½" floppy disk

Fig. 19. Floppy disks.

What is formatting all about?

Most floppy disks are bought pre-formatted. The initial **formatting** process prepares a disk to hold information. A **FAT** (**file allocation table**), which is a kind of menu system for the disk that keeps track of where all its files are placed, is also prepared. A used disk can be **quick-formatted** as a way of wiping it clean of its previous information. A quick format just renews the FAT so that the disk appears to be empty – when it is used again, any previous information is overwritten. This is how to format a floppy disk in Windows 95/98:

- Place the floppy disk in the drive, making sure it is not write protected.
- Double click on the my computer icon.
- Right click on the symbol **Floppy drive – A:**.
- Select **Format** from the menu.
- Choose the correct capacity.
- Make your choice of format.
- Click on **Start** as shown in Figure 20.

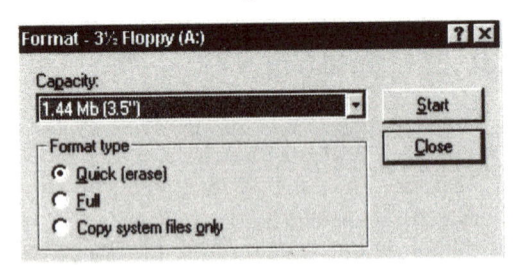

Fig. 20. The format dialogue box.

Installing a program from a floppy disk (Windows 95/98)

When you purchase a program on a floppy disk, it will have some sort of installation routine that does all the necessary work of transferring it from that floppy onto your hard drive. You just have to initiate that routine and confirm certain instructions along the way. Place the floppy into the A:\ drive, click on the start menu and select **Run**.

1. First you need to tell the computer where to find the initiation file. Type in **A:** at the **Open** command line, this makes the computer look to the floppy drive. Click on **Browse** – this will show you the available programs.

2. Look for the installation routine program. The most common names are **Setup** or **Install** but it may be something else such as **Autorun** or **Go**. Click to select it, then click on **Open**.

3. This takes you back to the run dialogue box but it will now have the full command line entered that it needs to install the program as seen in Figure 21. Click on OK and the program will begin to install.

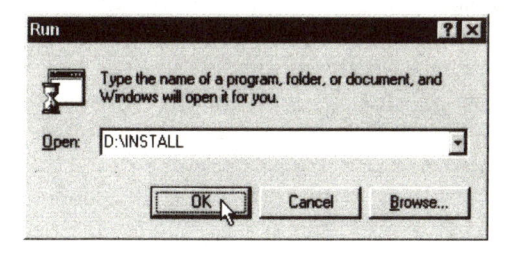

Fig. 21. The run dialogue box.

Confirming the installation instructions
There are so many different install routines that it would be impossible to explain them all. The most important thing to remember is to always read the screen. If the computer seems to come to a stop, there will probably be a question that is displayed on the screen waiting to be answered.

- Most routines need you to confirm on which drive you wish to install the program. Some already have the C:\ prompt there for you – this just requires you to confirm by pressing the enter key, or the Y key for yes. Others want you to press the corresponding letter key of your hard drive.

- At some time you will be shown which directory the program is going to install into. You will have the opportunity to change it. For example a game called Quake may advise you it will load into the **c:\quake** directory, you can change this to **c:\games\quake** if you wish.

- You may be required to enter a registration number. This will be on the paperwork that came with the disks. You may also be asked to agree to licensing laws that will be explained on the screen.

- If the program is on more than one disk, the installation routine will inform you when subsequent disks are required. Wait for the floppy drive light to go out, remove the disk and insert the next one. Press the enter key to continue.

Saving/copying files to a floppy disk (Windows 95/98)

Saving a file to a floppy disk can often be done directly from the program you are using. By choosing the save as command you can direct the program to save it to the A: drive. In some dialogue boxes this is shown as **Save in...** in the command line at the top of the window, as shown in Figure 22. Others will show it as the drives box towards the bottom of the dialogue box.

Copying files is easiest done in the Windows Explorer. Right click on the file you wish to copy and choose **send to...** from the menu. One of the options will be the floppy drive. Make sure a disk is inserted and click on this option. Windows Explorer will be covered in more detail in Chapter 8.

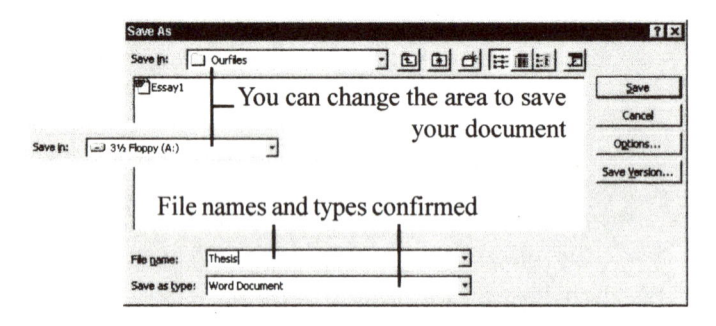

Fig. 22. Save as... dialogue box.

USING AND PLAYING CD-ROMS

CD-ROM stands for **compact disk read only memory**. They can store more than 600 megabytes of information – equivalent to more than 400 floppy disks. It is this that makes them an ideal medium for large programs. Files such as graphics, video and sound take up enormous amounts of space – often too much to store on floppy disks. This is why the majority of multimedia software is only available on CD-ROM.

What is multimedia?

It is the use of speech, music and video within a program. Most reference and educational software is multimedia. You will need a sound card, speakers and a CD-ROM to run multimedia software.

Understanding Your Disk Drives

A computer which is described as a multimedia system, will have these fitted.

Installing a program from a CD-ROM

The starting of an installation routine is the same as from a floppy disk with the exception of the drive letter. The CD-ROM is often the **D: drive**. There are, however, some differences once the install routine has started.

1. Some programs install all files that are required onto the hard drive. The program can then be run in the usual way from the menu – the CD may not have to be in the drive when the program is running.
2. Some programs enable you to make a choice.
   a) All files can be installed as in the option above.
   b) Some of the files can be installed – taking up less hard disk space but requiring the CD-ROM to be inserted for certain operations.
   c) A minimal installation that takes up the least amount of space on the hard disk but requires the CD to be inserted all the time the program is running. This can make the program slower in operation but if hard disk space is short then this is the one to choose.
3. Other programs such as encyclopaedias automatically install just the basic requirements to start the program and the CD has to be in the drive when running it.

For programs and installations that require the CD to be in the drive when they are running, you will benefit from having a faster CD-ROM drive.

DEFINING THE ROLE OF THE HARD DISK DRIVE

The hard disk drive is invisible to the user because it is inside the system unit. The only indication that it exists at all is a small light on the front of the system unit that flashes when the hard drive is in use.

Its first role is to store your operating system. After that it stores any further programs that you put onto it. The operating system also uses some of your hard drive space when running programs. Once a program is installed onto your hard drive it stays there until you remove it – even when you turn off your computer. Files on the hard drive can be accessed through the Windows explorer, which is explained in the following chapter.

Looking on the side of the packaging

Programs take up varying amounts of space. They usually give an indication as to how much is required on the side of the packaging. Graphics, video and sound orientated programs can take up large amounts of room and this includes most modern games. If you intend using these sorts of programs, then the bigger the hard drive the better, although having too big a hard drive can encourage you to fill it up with loads of rubbish you will probably very rarely use and will slow down your computer. The bigger the hard drive, the longer it takes your machine to search for files – but remember we are only talking about seconds. See the chapter on suggested system requirements for more details.

KEEPING YOUR COMPUTER HEALTHY

There are various ways to ensure the efficient running of your computer: placing it in a favourable position, keeping it clean, switching if off correctly. But just like a car, although you look after it carefully, every now and again it needs a service to keep the insides running sweetly. Your hard drive can become fragmented – bits of files here, there and everywhere slowing up the process of finding them when you start a program. The computer's menu system can become a little confused with continuous loading and deleting of programs and it can misplace clusters of information. Fortunately you don't need to take it apart or change the oil – all your maintenance can be done from the keyboard. You can check its condition and tidy it up with the operating systems tools known as **Scandisk** and **Defrag**.

Important differences between Windows 95/98 and Windows 3.11

In Windows 95/98, both of these tools can be found by pointing to **Programs, Accessories** and then **System Tools**. Run these programs only from that location, do not try to run them in DOS mode.

If they are not installed on your machine, you can add them from the original Windows 95/98 CD-ROM using the **Add/Remove Programs** in the control panel and selecting the **Windows Setup** tab – they are in **Disk Tools**.

In Windows 3.11, *do not* try to run them from within Windows. They can only be run from DOS. Close down Windows in the usual way, then at the DOS prompt type SCANDISK or DEFRAG. They should have been loaded in your DOS directory when the operating system was installed.

Understanding Your Disk Drives

Repairing with Scandisk

Scandisk – if the thorough test is chosen – will check all files and clusters on the hard drive for errors. If it reports any errors, it will make suggestions as to how these can be repaired and the majority of the time Scandisk will do this for you. If it completes the test with no errors, your computer's hard drive has a clean bill of health. It can be normal to have a few bad sectors on a hard drive. However, if these start increasing it is a sign of problems ahead, so consider buying a new hard drive.

Tidying up with Defrag

Windows 95 will often tell you that your system doesn't need defragmenting, as shown in Figure 23. However, you can do no harm by doing it anyway, quite the opposite. Windows 98 goes straight into the program, but by clicking on **settings** you can choose whether it rearranges your files to enable faster opening of programs or not. Sometimes referred to as **optimisation**, Defrag will reunite fragmented files and fill up any empty spaces that are dotted around on the hard drive. You can watch it working by clicking on **Show Details**. Depending on how fragmented your drive is, it may take anything from a few minutes to an hour or so to complete. Do not do this if there is any possibility of the electricity failing – your computer will be picking up and relocating files. If there is a power loss in the middle of this, some of the programs may end up with lost files.

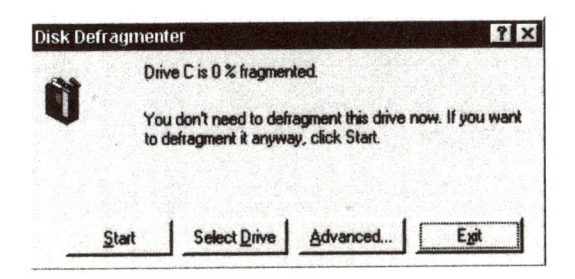

Fig. 23. Defrag start-up information.

Both these simple procedures will help you maintain your computer's good health and efficiency. Don't be put off if your computer takes a long time to run Defrag for the first time. If you perform this task regularly then it will not take long.

CASE STUDY

Lucy keeps things running smoothly

Following on from her success with the file structure, Lucy is elected by the family to keep the computer in healthy working order. She accomplishes this by running the defragmentation routine from the system tools menu each Monday morning after the weekend's computer-bashing sessions, in which the children load on and delete their various game demos. She has found that by establishing a regular routine for this it takes only a few minutes.

PRACTICAL EXERCISE

See how big your hard drive is. People often ask 'How big is your hard drive?' or you may want to know how much space you have left – is it enough to load a particular program that you have just purchased?

- Double click on the my computer icon.
- Right click on the C: drive displayed.
- Left click on the properties selection.
- You will now have a display showing how big your hard drive is and a graphical image showing how much space you have left, as shown in Figure 24.

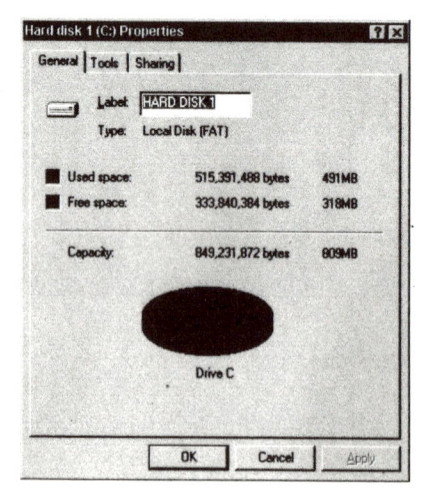

Fig. 24. Hard disk properties dialogue box.

8
Organising Your Computer with Windows 95/98

Chapter 4 looked at the appearance of Windows 95/98. This chapter will explain the significance of Windows as an operating system and how it assists you in running the other programs you have installed on your machine.

SEEING WHERE IT IS ALL STORED – THE EXPLORER

Explorer allows you to view all folders and files stored on your hard disk, floppy disk or CD-ROM. It displays a tree structure as explained in Chapter 6. There are at least three ways to open explorer:

1. Click on the start menu, point to programs and select explorer.

2. Right click on the my computer icon and select explorer from the menu.

3. If you have a Windows 95 keyboard, press the windows symbol and the E key at the same time.

You can move, copy, add and delete items in explorer and for these reasons please exercise caution. A computer can become very confused if certain files are moved or disappear altogether. Always read the messages the computer prompts you with when you are about to do something and double-check that it is doing what you intended!

Explaining the layout
The explorer window has two parts, as shown in Figure 25. The left side shows the tree structure of your computer, the right side shows what is stored *underneath* the highlighted selection of the left panel.

Small plus and minus symbols next to the folders enable movement through the tree structure without actually selecting the folders. It makes working through the tree a little quicker, because

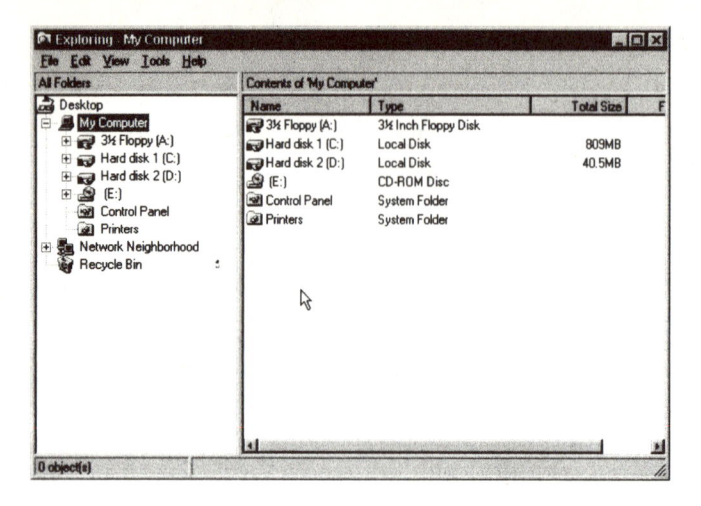

Fig. 25. Windows 95 explorer window.

each time you select a folder the computer looks to see what is inside it and displays this in the right panel. If you don't actually select the folder, just use the plus sign to open up the tree; the right side does not have to be updated.

- The **View** menu can be used to customise the way explorer displays its contents. Selecting **Details** offers the most information in an easy to decipher manner.
- The **File** menu can be used to add new folders to the tree structure. Click your mouse where you wish to insert a new folder, choose **file, new, folder** and give it a name.

Looking at your hard drive

By selecting the C: you can view what is on your hard drive. In Figure 26, which shows a Windows 98 web style window, after selecting the hard drive the plus signs were then used to open up the Killaton folder. Any of you that have the Game Duke Nukem (Atomic version) on your PC will recognise this. In it, a sub-folder called Atomic was selected. This displays its contents in the right panel, which consists of further sub-folders plus some files. Once a plus sign has been clicked on to expand the tree, it changes to a minus sign. Clicking on this will reverse the operation.

What use is this to me?

One example is perhaps to create your own **clipart** folder to store

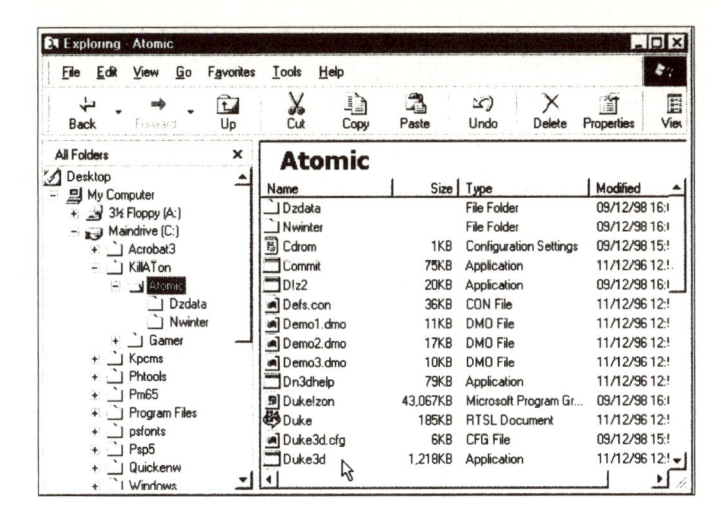

Fig. 26. Showing the explorer tree structure.

many of the free clipart samples that come on the cover disks of computer magazines.

1. Highlight the C: drive. You place your new folder here in the root.
2. Select file, new, folder and click. A new folder will appear, call it Clipart.
3. Highlight your new Clipart folder in the left panel. You can now add a sub-folder.
4. Repeat instruction number two but this time call your folder Cartoons.
5. Any cartoon clipart that you come across can be copied into this folder and is kept neatly together.

In the future, if you decide to remove this folder from your hard drive, highlight it with your mouse, right click and select *delete* to remove it.

Copying and moving files around
Files and folders can be moved or copied using the **Cut** and **Paste** commands. The difference between moving and copying seems obvious but the terms can sometimes be confused. Copying makes a copy of the item, leaving the original files in place. Moving moves the files from one place to another.

Have a go!
Using the example of the clipart folder, copy some files from a disk to the cartoon folder.

- Insert the CD-ROM or floppy disk containing the files you wish to copy.
- Using explorer, locate the folder containing these files and highlight it.
- Select the files using your mouse. Multiple files can be selected by holding down the shift key on your keyboard at the same time as selecting the files with your mouse.
- Right click the mouse button and choose **Copy**.

At this stage nothing seems to have happened – but it has. The files you selected to copy have been copied onto the computer clipboard ready for pasting. Go back to the hard drive, open up the clipart folder and select the cartoon folder. Right click on this and select **Paste**. The files will begin copying into that folder.

LOADING A NEW PROGRAM

There are two methods of loading a new program in Windows 95/98. The first, using the run command, was covered in the previous chapter. The alternative way is using the **add/remove programs** icon in control panel. This has an install button that automatically searches, first the floppy disk, then the CD-ROM for any relevant installation programs.

You may be asked some simple questions, such as where you wish to load your new program. More often than not, a suggestion will be made that leaves you to just press the enter key on your keyboard if you agree.

Removing programs

Programs can be removed in explorer by selecting the relevant folder and choosing delete from the right click. However, some programs on installation deposit files in other areas such as your windows system directory. Removing the programs in this way leaves these residual files lingering in your system and taking up valuable room. The solution to this is to use the Windows **uninstaller** facility that can ensure they are removed completely. The **add/remove programs** icon in control panel lists the programs it can delete correctly. Highlight your choice and click on the add/remove button to start the process. See Figure 27.

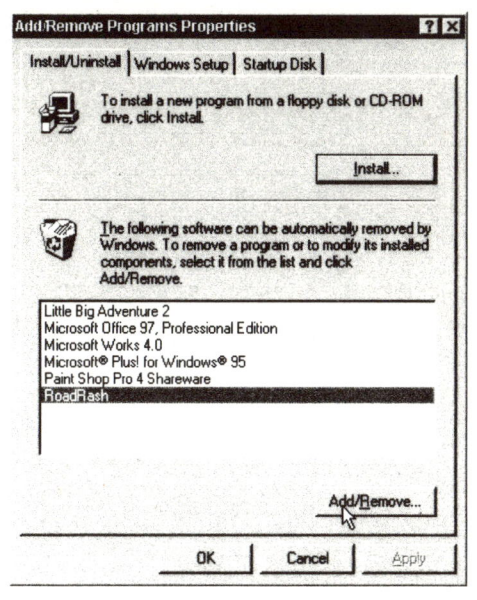

Fig. 27. Add/remove programs dialogue box.

ADDING AND REMOVING ENTRIES FROM THE MENU

Many programs add a menu entry into Windows for you to access it. Often when removing programs, the uninstaller removes these entries. There will be times, however, when you will have to do this yourself. Removing an entry from the menu does not remove the program from your hard disk drive, just from the menu system. Similarly, if you have just loaded a program and there is no reference to it in the menu system, it doesn't mean it hasn't loaded properly – just that you will have to add the menu entry yourself. These problems occur when software was not originally written specifically for Windows 95 or Windows 98.

Select **Settings** from the start menu, click on task bar, and then choose the **Start Menu Programs** tab. There are three options, as shown in Figure 28: to add, to remove and the other is for advanced users.

Adding a menu entry

A **command line** needs to be entered. This means the path to the program that you wish to add into the menu. Have a go at adding a calculator menu entry, then removing it in a moment.

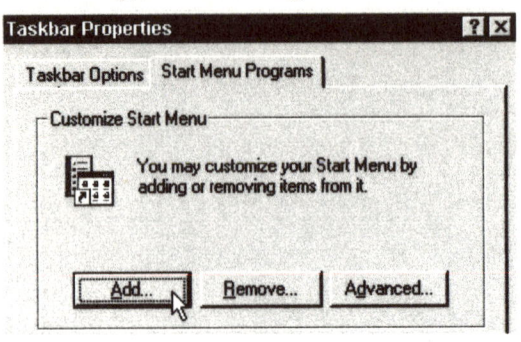

Fig. 28. Task bar properties box.

- After pressing the **Add** button, click on **Browse**. Double click on the Windows folder then scroll along until you find the **Calc** file and double click on it. This will have entered the command line to the calculator program that is stored in the Windows folder.

- Click on **Next**. Now you have to say where you wish the entry to be. Try creating your own sub-group of **accessories**. Click on accessories once, then on new folder; type in **Essentials**.

- Click on next. The name you enter here is exactly how it will appear in the menu, let's call it Adding Machine, and click on **Finish**.

Now go to your start menu, point to accessories, you should see your new group called essentials. Point to that and click on adding machine to start the calculator.

Removing a menu entry

Click on **Remove** and look for the item you wish to delete. To delete the above entry, click on the plus sign at the side of accessories to open up the tree. Highlight essentials and click on remove. You will be asked to confirm that you wish to delete this entry; click on **Close** and your entry is gone.

Windows 98 differences
Items can also be added to the menu in both Windows 95 and 98 by selecting the program or file from within Explorer, then dragging and dropping it onto the Menu Start button. This places the file at the top of the first menu, above Programs.

In Windows 98, you can then select this again, and by holding down the mouse button and dragging the selection across the menu system, you can position it exactly where you wish. It is also possible to remove a selection by right clicking it and choosing delete from the menu.

CASE STUDY

Beverly does some housekeeping
Beverly has joined the computer club at school and regularly swaps CDs featuring demonstration programs with other members of the group. Her parents have told her that the fly-out menu system is becoming clogged up with entries for games that she has since deleted. If she doesn't remove these items from the menus, then in future she will not be allowed to install them.

With the help files for guidance she uses the relevant section of the task bar properties to remove any redundant menu entries.

PRACTICAL EXERCISE

This exercise will show you how to back up saved files from your hard disk onto a floppy disk. If this is done on a regular basis, and your computer ever goes wrong, you will not lose all your work. If your drive is reformatted, you would load the programs back on, then copy your files from floppy disk back onto the hard drive and you are back to where you were before it went wrong.

1. Put a floppy disk into the drive, ensuring it is not write protected.

2. Open Windows explorer and highlight the folder where your files are stored.

3. Select your files in one of the following ways:
   - Individually by clicking on them with the mouse button.
   - In a group, by selecting the first file, then hold down the shift

key on your keyboard and select the last file – all files in between will be selected.

- Random files, by holding the **Ctrl** key on your keyboard and selecting each file in turn while still holding down the key.

4. While all your files are selected, click on the right mouse button.

5. Point to the **Send To** command in the menu, and click on A: floppy drive.

6. Your files will now begin copying.

Points to note
If any files that you attempt to copy are close to or more than 1.44megabytes – the size of the floppy disk – they will not fit. Watch the command line at the bottom of the explorer window, which will show you how many files are selected and their collective size.

If a single file is more than this size, it cannot be copied onto floppy disk using this method. You must use the **Backup** feature which splices the file. You can learn about this in the help files.

9
Organising Your Computer with Windows 3.11

If you are running Windows 3.11 many procedures are similar to those in Windows 95/98, so please do refer to that chapter. Here, we will consider and explain those areas in which the differences occur.

Programs are stored in directories and sub-directories in Windows 3.11, as opposed to folders in Windows 95/98. These are the same items, just a different name. **Program Manager** is the first window you will see and it is from here that you can access and run all other programs.

Windows 3.11 is not a complete operating system in itself. It needs the DOS program (disk operating system) as well. The two work side by side.

SEEING WHERE IT IS ALL STORED – THE FILE MANAGER

The **File Manager** icon can be found in the window called **Main**. Double click on this to open it. It does the same job as explorer in Windows 95/98 but has a few differences in the way it operates. On opening, you will be looking at your hard drive's content: refer to Figure 29. Underneath the title bar is the **drive bar** that has a small graphical image of each of your drives with their relevant letter next to them. If you wish to look at the contents of a different drive, click on its icon.

Providing the **Indicate Expandable Branches** has been ticked in the **Tree** menu, the plus and minus signs that indicate if a directory has sub-directories are shown on the directories themselves. This means that if you wish to expand the tree structure, the relevant directory has to be double clicked. This action automatically highlights this directory which in turn displays its contents in the right panel. File manger shows the name of all files in the selected directory, along with their extensions. You can change the way you view these details from the view menu.

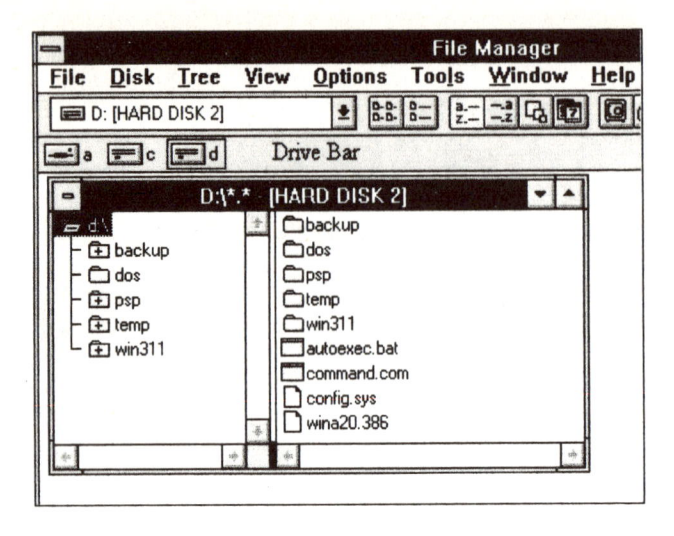

Fig. 29. Windows 3.11 file manager window.

Performing the changes
The cut and paste commands cannot be used in file manager, but it is a simple task to open two windows and drag files and directories from one place to another. For example, if you wish to copy a file from a floppy disk to the hard drive this can be done using the following method:

- Open file manager and make sure you can see the directory that you wish to copy the files into.

- Insert the floppy disk and *double click* on the A: drive icon in the drive bar. Double clicking creates a second window.

- In this second window, select the files you wish to copy. Hold down the mouse button and drag them to the selected directory in the other window.

- Let go of the mouse button and the files will begin copying.

Figure 30 shows how the two windows are displayed. You can see that the mouse pointer has a small icon indicating the files being carried over.

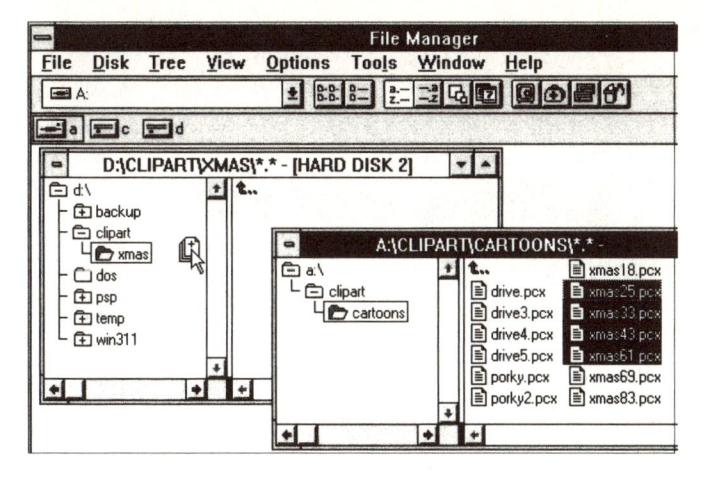

Fig. 30. Copying files from one window to another.

Using the disk menu
If you need to copy or format a floppy disk, this can be accomplished using the **Disk** menu. The copy command reads the information from the original disk and will then ask you to remove it and insert the destination disk. Pressing the enter key begins the process of writing the files onto the new disk.

The **Format** command, as explained in Chapter 7, asks you to confirm the drive you wish to format and the size of the disk. Click OK to begin the process.

LOADING A NEW PROGRAM

With the program manager window open, click on the **File** menu and select the **Run** command. The rest of the procedure is the same as for Windows 95/98.

Removing a program
Windows 3.11 does not have the automatic facility to add and remove programs. Separate uninstaller programs can be purchased that will enable you to remove programs in the correct manner. Using these will ensure that your Windows system files do not become full of redundant information.

If you do not have an uninstaller, programs must be removed by highlighting the relevant directory in the file manager and pressing the delete key on your keyboard.

ADDING AND REMOVING ICONS FROM THE GROUPS

When a program is installed, it will usually create its own group or window with all the necessary icons inside. If it doesn't, and you wish to create your own, refer to the section Creating New Windows and Icons in Chapter 5.

Programs that are not designed to run in Windows will certainly not install a group or an icon. This does not necessarily mean that they cannot be run from Windows, only trying them will tell you.

To remove an icon, single click on it with the mouse button to highlight, then press the delete key on your keyboard. Removing a window/group is exactly the same, however you cannot delete it unless it is empty of icons. Remember – removing an icon does not remove the actual program from the computer, just its icon.

CASE STUDY

Finding more and more uses

Jean has become interested in Eric's new hobby. Whilst attending her weekly diet club meeting, she discovers that they sell a computer disk containing recipes for their diet plan. She buys the disk, and takes it home to Eric and asks him to show her how to install it. Eric sits Jean down at the computer and talks her through the installation process using file manager to find and launch the install routine.

Jean is thrilled with the program and notices that the recipes can be printed out to use in the kitchen. Eric resigns himself to the fact that he is now going to have to buy a printer.

PRACTICAL EXERCISE

Floppy disks can become damaged more easily than CD-ROMs. They are sensitive to heat, radiation and magnetism. It is always a good idea to have a back up copy of floppy disks in case one gets damaged. Use the following instructions to make a copy of an original floppy disk.

1. Write protect the original disk by opening the tab. This will ensure you do not accidentally overwrite onto it.

2. Put the disk into the floppy drive and open the file manager.

3. From the disk menu just underneath the title bar select **copy disk**.

4. A warning sign tells you that all data on the destination disk will be erased. Ensure you are using either a blank destination disk, or one that doesn't have any files on that you do not wish to lose. Click yes to continue.

5. A sign tells you to insert the source disk. Click on OK when you are ready to copy.

6. The computer is now reading the information from the original disk. You will see the light on the front of the floppy drive and a dialogue box will show the percentage that has been completed.

7. When it reaches 49%, you will be asked to insert the destination disk. Remove the original after the light has gone out and insert the other disk. Click OK.

8. The percentage sign will go all the way up to 100% and return you to file manager. Your disk is now copied; label it and put it somewhere safe.

10
Looking at Programs for Correspondence

Correspondence is one of the main reasons given for buying a computer. The definition of correspondence has been stretched slightly in this chapter to include any written document intended to convey a message. You will be using word processor and desktop publishing programs, which will enable you to produce professional looking letters, leaflets, posters and a host of other documents. So, what are the advantages of using a computer instead of writing by hand or using a typewriter?

- Your work can be saved and printed later.
- You can change things around at any time.
- There is no possibility of someone not being able to read your handwriting.
- The computer can check your spelling and grammar.
- You can use different sizes and styles to improve its appearance.
- You can print as many copies as you want.
- You will definitely save money on correction fluid.

With these programs you can do anything from producing your own stationery to publishing your own magazine. In this chapter you will learn the basics, plus a few tips to set you on the right road.

CREATING LETTERS WITH WORD PROCESSING

Typing onto a screen instead of a piece of paper does not come naturally. When you first open your word processor it may look a little daunting, new programs do to all of us. Word processors vary slightly from one to another but they all contain similar features. We will look at some of these in more detail and later you can try them out in the practical exercise at the end of the chapter.

Understanding the screen

Figure 31 shows a large blank area in the middle of the screen – this

Looking at Programs for Correspondence

is your paper. You may see some figures along the top and down the left side, these are ruler markings to assist you when lining up areas of text. Above the blank area is the **tool bar**. This is a set of icons that allow shortcuts to various actions such as saving or printing your files. Above the tool bar will be a row of **menu selections**. These can be clicked on with the mouse to give you a further drop-down menu that will make various other functions available.

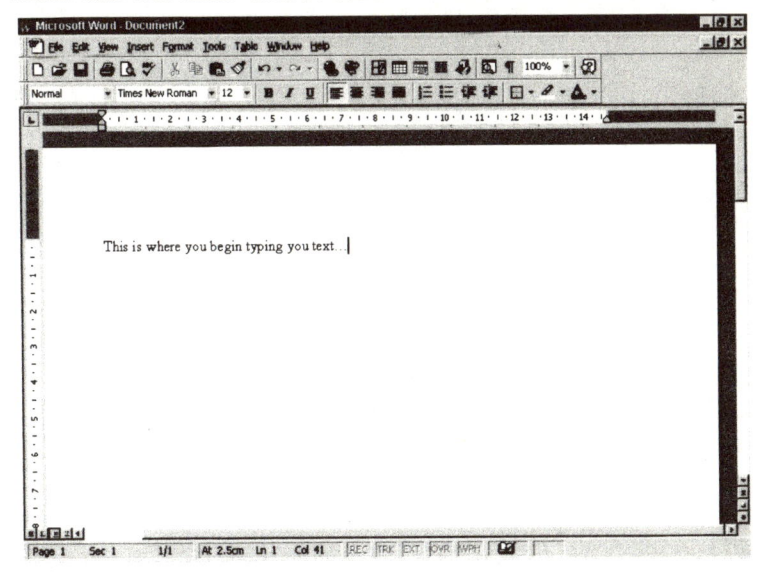

Fig. 31. Word processor screen.

Searching through the menu selections

The most popular title descriptions include: **File, Edit, Format, Tools, Window** and **Help**. Each one provides a range of functions and even though the names may vary from program to program they will normally fall into the following groups.

File
This provides a list of actions relating to your file. From this menu you can start a new file, open an existing file, save and print a file, or close a file. Often you will also find the set-up options for your page in this menu.

Edit
These commands enable you to edit or change the way your text or layout looks. Once you have selected the items you wish to change,

you can choose to cut the relevant piece out, copy it, replace it or undo the last change that you made.

Format
Do not confuse this with the **Disk Format** command. In this sense it refers to the way your text will look. You can change its typeface, make it bold or bigger, italicise or underline it from this menu. You can give instructions as to how the layout will appear – how many spaces between paragraphs, whether you want borders around your work, add bullets or place your text into columns, etc.

Tools
Using the options in this menu you can check the spelling and grammar in your document. You can sometimes do a word count and join two documents together – called **merging**. You may also be able to print envelopes and labels from here.

Window
This menu shows you which document is selected at present. If you have more than one document open at a time, you can also change from one to the other using this menu. You can even see both documents at the same time using the **Split** or **Tile** command.

Help
Probably the most useful menu of them all when you are new to a program. This allows you access to the program's help files. You should have a choice of searching for a particular topic, looking at general contents, or doing a tutorial on the program itself.

A word about wrapping
If you are used to using a typewriter, the concept of **word wrapping** may seem strange at first. With a typewriter you have to press the carriage return at the end of each line to start typing on the next line. A word processor does this for you. Once you have set up the page to the desired margin widths and begin typing, the text will start at the left margin, when it reaches the right margin it will automatically start a new line. Later on, if you should add, delete or alter any text, the program will automatically **re-wrap** your document, moving text around as necessary to ensure you have complete lines.

Of course, if you wish to end a line early, such as the end of a paragraph, or with a short sentence, you can simply press the return

Looking at Programs for Correspondence

key on your keyboard and this puts you onto the next line. This is known as a **hard return**.

Changing your page set-up
All documents have a default page setting. This is the way that your 'page' appears every time you start your word processor. Most of the time the default settings will suit your needs, other times you will want to change them. The options will include the following:

Page orientation
This is selecting whether you want your page to be vertical or horizontal. The default is usually vertical. Other terms used for vertical/horizontal are portrait/landscape, tall/wide.

Page size
The default for this size is usually A4 as this suits most printers. Other options may include A5, B5, letter, legal, envelope or your own custom size.

Margin size
The defaults here can vary tremendously from program to program, but are normally in the region of 1in/2.5cms all the way around the page. Measurements can be set individually for the top, bottom, right and left margins. When setting the measurements, remember that most printers have a limit as to how close to the edge of the paper they can print. The printer needs a little space to hold the paper while it is feeding it through its rollers. As a guide, don't set your margins below ½in or 13mm.

Where to make the changes
Page Setup is normally found in the file drop-down menu just below the title bar.

Other commands on the file menu
The first two commands available on the file drop-down menu are normally **New** and **Open Existing File**. Further down you may find **Save, Save as, Print, Print Preview, Exit** or **Close**.

New
Use this when you wish to start a new document. If you have made a hash of a previous one and want to start again, you can click on this command and it gives you a new page. If your word processor

doesn't automatically start with the blank page in front of you, this is where you will find it.

Open existing file
If you have a previously named and saved file that you want to open, you would choose this command. You are presented with a dialogue box similar to the one shown in Figure 32. In this box you tell the computer where to find your file, what it is called and instruct the program to open it.

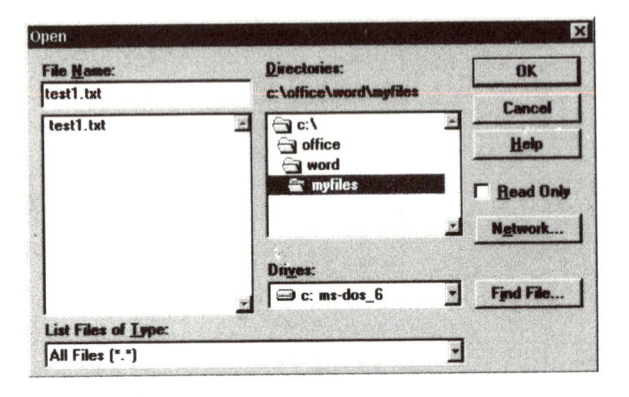

Fig. 32. The open file dialogue box.

The dialogue box will have an area for you to tell the computer where to look for your file. This may be labelled **Look In...** or **Drives**. The dialogue box will usually be showing the C drive, which is your hard drive. It may also be showing the directory or folder where your documents are stored.

- Microsoft products such as Office 97 have a default setting of storing all personally created files in the **My Documents** folder. They have now extended this to Windows 98 and many other programs are following suit.

- To open a file from another drive, such as the floppy drive, click on the arrow by the drive box and select A:\drive.

When you have correctly located the file you wish to open, click on it and choose the OK button.

Save
This command is used when you are ready to save your work to

Looking at Programs for Correspondence

disk, whether it is to the hard drive or floppy disk. This presents you with a similar dialogue box to the one mentioned above. The difference is that you now have to tell the computer what you want to call the file, and where to put it. Make sure you have selected the correct drive and directory in which you wish to store the file. In the file box enter the name you want to give your work.

In Windows 3.11 you are limited to filenames consisting of no more than eight characters. Since the introduction of Windows 95 you are not limited to this. However, if you are giving someone else the file to use on another computer, consider what version of Windows they may be using. If the other computer has Windows 3.11, keep your name to a maximum of eight characters. A useful tip when naming files is to call them something that will remind you what it is about. This will help find the correct file again much more easily, especially if you are looking for it some months later. To find out more about naming files, refer to Chapter 6.

Save as...
This differs from the save command in the following way. If you have already saved a file using the save command, each time you use save thereafter it will overwrite the file already created. Using the save as command gives you the option to rename your work. Giving it a slightly different name will then save a second copy and preserve the original.

Print and print preview
Clicking on these commands enables you to see in advance how your document will appear once it is printed. This is covered in the later section of Previewing and Printing Your Work.

Close or exit
This closes the program that you are working in. Some programs give the option to close just the document window – leaving the actual program still running, ready to start a new document. If you have not already saved your work, the program will prompt you to do so before closing itself, as shown in Figure 33.

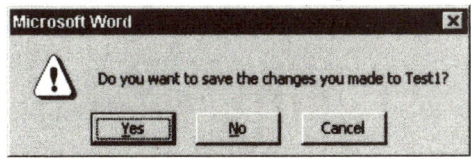

Fig. 33. Confirming information dialogue box.

Describing formatting terms
It is necessary to understand some of the formatting terms that you will be using so here is a brief introduction to some of them.

Bold
This will emphasise text by giving it a heavier appearance, making it stand out – ie not bolded – **bolded**.

Justification
This adjusts the alignment of your work.

> **Left justification** means that all text will start and line up at the left margin – the right side will be jagged.

> **Right justification** means all text will end and line up on the right margin – the left side will be jagged.

> **Centred** means that all text will appear equal distance from both left and right margins.
> Both the right and left sides will be jagged.

> **Full justification** means that both the left and right margins will line up neatly. The processor puts in automatic spacing throughout the lines to ensure this happens.

Font
This is the type of writing that you are using, known as the **typeface**. Two of the most common fonts are Times New Roman and Arial. If you look closely you can see the differences.

> This is a sample of Times New Roman.
> **This is a sample of Arial.**

Font size
Sometimes referred to as **point size**. The higher the point the larger the letters.

> This is font size twelve.
> ## This is font size twenty.

Cut
This is when you highlight part of your document and move it from its current position. The computer temporarily holds the highlighted part on its built-in clipboard ready for you to place it into its new position. Highlights and selecting will be covered later in the chapter.

Copy
This takes just a copy of a highlighted section, leaving the selected part in place. The copied part is held on the clipboard for you to copy to another area of your document.

Paste
This is the act of placing your selected item from the clipboard into its new position in your document.

All these are printing terms left over from the days when editors had to literally cut things out and paste them elsewhere to change a layout prior to publication.

So how do I actually use a word processor?

When using a typewriter you had to decide how you wanted your work to look before you typed it. With a word processor you type it in first, then smarten it up afterwards.

While typing in your text, if you realise you need to **add** a word in the middle of a sentence, just click the mouse cursor at the spot you wish to enter the word, then type. Your word will be slotted in and the rest of the text will move along to allow for it. Similarly, if you wish to **remove** a word, again go to the beginning of the word you wish to delete and click with the mouse so that your cursor is in position – then press the delete key and watch your word disappear letter by letter.

You can delete things a little quicker by **selecting** the whole word or sentence and pressing the **delete** key. To find out how to select things read on...

IMPROVING THE LAYOUT IN AN INSTANT

This is where you can begin having fun with a word processor. You can move bits from one place to another – add words, change sentences, emphasise important words or titles all with the click of a mouse.

I've typed my text in, now how do I do all these things?

To use any of the functions available in a word processor you first have to select the part you wish to change. This tells the computer program what you wish to work with. If you don't select or **highlight** anything it doesn't know what you want it to do.

To select something, click the mouse where you wish your selection to begin, then while holding down the mouse button, drag the cursor to the end of the selection and release the button. You will be able to see that this area is now highlighted, because the text will appear white on a black background as shown in Figure 34.

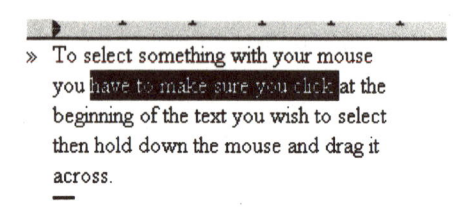

> » To select something with your mouse you have to make sure you click at the beginning of the text you wish to select then hold down the mouse and drag it across.

Fig. 34. Highlighted text.

Using shortcut methods

With many programs you can speed up this process by highlighting a whole paragraph. Place your mouse cursor at the beginning of the paragraph, to the left side of the first line. Your cursor may change to an arrow pointing at the text. Hold down the mouse button and drag in a downward direction. The highlight will automatically select each whole line in turn. By placing the cursor within a word and double clicking, the whole word will be selected. Triple clicking within any word selects that complete line.

I've selected my area of text, now how do I change it?

Select the command you wish to use from the menus. The commands that are most regularly used are often given a shortcut by way of an icon on the tool bar. Now you have selected the area you wish to change, just click on the appropriate command. Figure 35 shows some of the icons found on the tool bar in the **Microsoft Word** program. Below is a brief description of their uses.

i   Changes the text to bold when you click on it.

ii Changes the writing to italics.

iii Underlines the selected text.

Looking at Programs for Correspondence 83

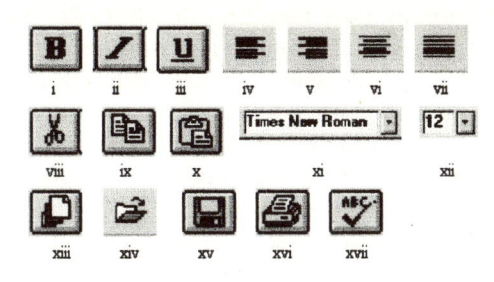

Fig. 35. Sample icons in programs.

Click on any of the icons a second time to return the text to its original stage.

iv Ensures that your text is left justified.

v   Ensures that it will be right justified.

vi Justifies the text from the centre.

vii Gives full justification on both sides.

As you click on each one in turn you will see your text change accordingly, so you can decide which looks best before clicking your mouse again to deselect the text.

viii This enables you to cut the selection, removing it from its present position. Once you have done this, click your cursor at the new point and use the paste command.

ix   This copies the piece of text you have selected onto the clipboard. Use the same procedure as the cut command to paste the copy into the new position.

x   This icon is used in conjunction with the cut and copy commands to 'paste' the selection into its new position.

xi   Displays the font that is presently in use. Clicking on the arrow at the right side enables you to choose from other fonts available. To select the one you need, click on it with your mouse.

xii Displays the font size. Again, clicking on the arrow shows you other available sizes to select.

Looking at other icons

The way in which tool bars and icons are displayed varies from program to program. However, they usually have descriptive pictures on them. This chapter will help you understand what to look for, even if your word processor differs from that above. Here are the other descriptions to the remaining icons in Figure 35.

xiii Starts a new page. Clicking on this has the same effect as choosing the file menu, then selecting new.

xiv This will display the dialogue box to open an existing file.

xv This will save the current document. If this is the first time you have saved the file, a dialogue box will be displayed for you to name and place your file. Subsequent use will merely update this file.

xvi Sends a copy of your document for printing.

xvii Starts that wonderful invention for checking your spelling – this is covered later under its own heading.

There are many more icons that may be shown on your tool bar. Quite often programs have a way of telling you what each icon represents. By holding your mouse pointer over one of the icons for a couple of seconds, it will give you a brief description of what that icon does. If you are unsure of an icon's meaning, use the help file found on the menu bar. These days the help files are of more use than the manuals and handbooks that come packaged with a program – if you get any manuals!

DESIGNING WITH DESKTOP PUBLISHING

Although many word processors allow you to use pictures, shading, borders, etc, there is less flexibility with regard to positioning. than there is with a desktop publisher. A desktop publisher is designed specifically to allow the free use of these facilities in any way you choose. However the difference between the two is getting smaller all the time.

Explaining the differences

Word processors work in lines – for example, you start at the top of the page and work your way down. If you wanted to start halfway down the page in a word processor, you would have to enter a series

Looking at Programs for Correspondence 85

of blank lines to get to the area you wished to start at.

With a desktop publisher you work with the whole page. Everything is based around frames that can be placed anywhere on the page, even on top of each other. For example, if you have a page that has writing, a picture and a border all the way around, each one of these 'bits' would be a separate item. The picture may be on top of the writing with the writing flowing each side neatly, but each item is on a different layer. Figure 36 has three layers: the border will be in one layer, the writing in a second and the third contains the picture. Layering is covered in more detail later in the chapter.

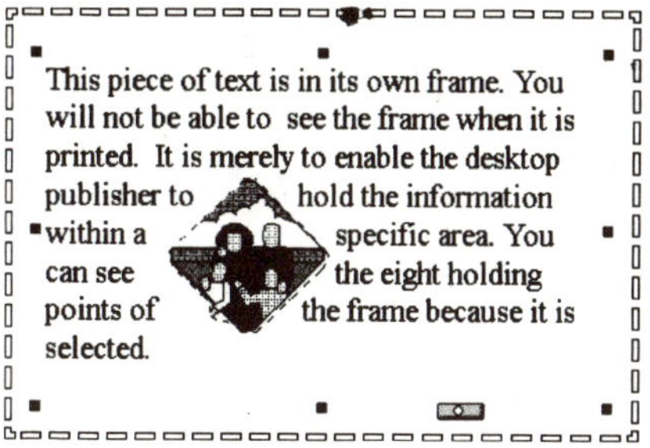

This piece of text is in its own frame. You will not be able to see the frame when it is printed. It is merely to enable the desktop publisher to hold the information within a specific area. You can see the eight holding points of the frame because it is selected.

Fig. 36. Desktop publishing facilities.

Working with wizards and templates

Wizards and **templates** are pre-constructed layouts that enable you to add your own information and create a piece of work in a fraction of the time it would take starting from scratch. The kinds of templates a desktop publisher may provide are:

- make your own greetings cards
- produce your own newsletter
- create your own cassette tape inserts
- design your own calendar
- create your own invoice/quotation/order form
- print your own business cards and letterheads
- make big banners for your parties.

Understanding layers

This is an important principle to understand. In Figure 37 there are three layers, each holding a different shape. In the first diagram the arrow is on the top layer, the rectangle in the middle and the circle on the bottom. The layers could be rearranged by clicking on the arrow to select it and choosing **Send to Back** from the **Arrange** menu. Then you could click on the circle and use the same procedure with **Bring to Front**. In the second diagram the arrow is now on the bottom layer and the circle on the top. Think of the three shapes as being separate pieces of paper that you can shuffle around. That is layering.

This concept of layering is used when you wish to place a picture inside a piece of text. In a desktop publisher this is easily done because of the layering technique; the text and the picture are not occupying the same space – they are merely one on top of the other. In Microsoft Publisher, the writing automatically moves so that the picture does not obscure it. In other programs it may be necessary to use the text-wrapping tool so that the picture will repel text.

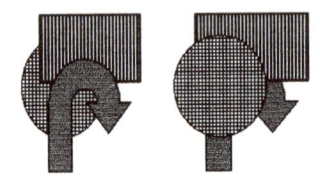

Fig. 37. Explaining layers.

When would you use the cropping tool?
The cropping tool is used to adjust the shape of the picture's frame and make your text fit even more snugly. You can see the difference in a picture frame that is not cropped, and one that is, with the two bananas in Figure 38. The first banana has an imaginary square frame around it to which the text fits. The second banana has had the square frame cropped around the shape of the actual banana, so the writing can sit closer.

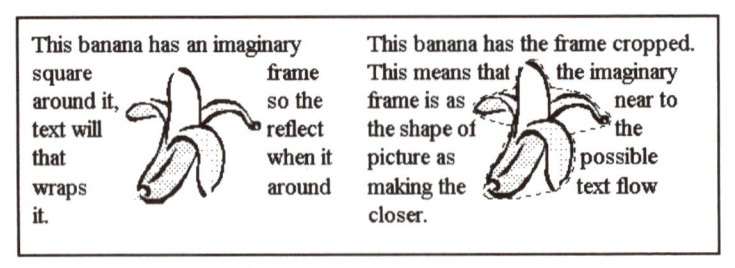

This banana has an imaginary square around it, text will that wraps it.	frame so the reflect when it around	This banana has the frame cropped. This means that the imaginary frame is as near to the shape of the picture as possible making the text flow closer.

Fig. 38. Showing picture cropping.

ADDING THAT SPECIAL LOOK

Amongst the many other options available are the facilities to add borders, shading and shadows, fancy first letters of paragraphs – in fact, whole sentences can be constructed in fancy ways. In order to make your work attractive you should limit the number of typefaces to two on any one page. Check out the leaflets that come through your door and see what looks good.

Again, as with a word processor, anything you want to change or add a special look to first needs to be selected. Do this by clicking on the object you wish to play with. Once selected, look through the menus to find the command you wish to use, or use the shortcut icon. This is great fun and children from 7 to 70 will spend hours changing things around and experimenting.

Another useful facility found in most word processors these days as well as desktop publishers is the ability to rotate text so that it can appear diagonally across the page – or even from top to bottom.

Creating some fancy stuff

1. To create the box of text in Figure 39, select a blank full page. Create a **text box** by clicking on the **text tool** at the left side of the screen. Draw a frame with the mouse cursor, remembering to hold the mouse button down to draw the frame. This 'box' will not print out on the final copy – it is merely a guide frame that holds the text inside.

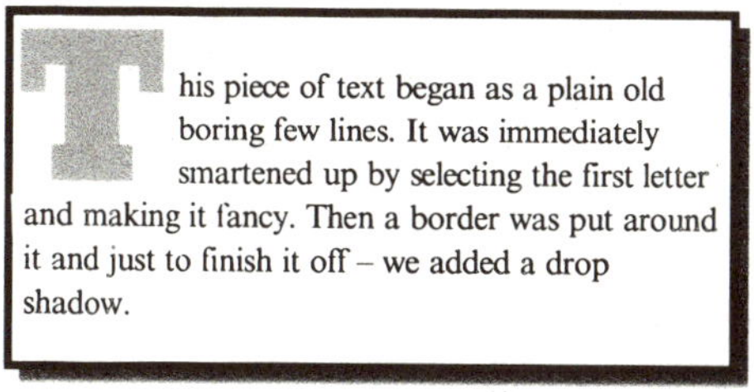

   > **T**his piece of text began as a plain old boring few lines. It was immediately smartened up by selecting the first letter and making it fancy. Then a border was put around it and just to finish it off – we added a drop shadow.

   Fig. 39. More desktop publishing features.

2. Type in your words and highlight the first letter only of the first paragraph. Click on the format menu underneath the title bar and choose **Fancy First Letter**. You are then given a choice of different shaped letters and positions in which it can be placed. Make your choice and click on OK.

3. Next, make sure you re-select the frame that the text is in. Then from the format menu choose **Borders**. After making your choice there, click on the icon showing a white square with a shadow at the extreme right of the tool bar, which is the shortcut icon to add a drop shadow to your border.

HAVING YOUR WORK CHECKED BY THE SPELLCHECKER

The spellchecker can be found in one of the menus below the title bar. In Microsoft Word, for instance, it is the first command in the tools menu and is described as **Spelling and Grammar**. Many programs also have a shortcut icon on the tool bar which is most often pictured with the letters ABC on it.

To check a document, make sure that your cursor is at the start of the text, otherwise the spellchecker will begin wherever the cursor is, consequently missing some areas near the beginning. Click on the command and away it goes.

What setting up is needed?

Setting it up usually involves making sure it is using the correct language. For example, if it is set up for American English, it would see the spelling of 'color' as correct. If it is set up for British English, it will suggest that you change this spelling to 'colour'.

If your spellchecker does not allow you to change the language in the spellchecker dialogue box, you may need to use the program set-up options. In Microsoft Works, for example, you have to close down the initial start-up screen. To do this click cancel then click on the tools menu and select options. In the dialogue box change the speller from American to British English.

Getting the checker to do the work for you

Some programs automatically give you an alternative spelling suggestion, see an example of this in Figure 40, other programs need setting up first. This will normally be quite plain when you first start the checker. In Microsoft Works, for example, there is a checkbox for you to mark if you wish it to make suggestions to you.

How the spellchecker works

The programs have a built in dictionary. How many words, or how good it is, will depend on the program you are using. In general, the more expensive the program, the better the dictionary and grammar check will be. It checks each word of your document and as soon as

Looking at Programs for Correspondence

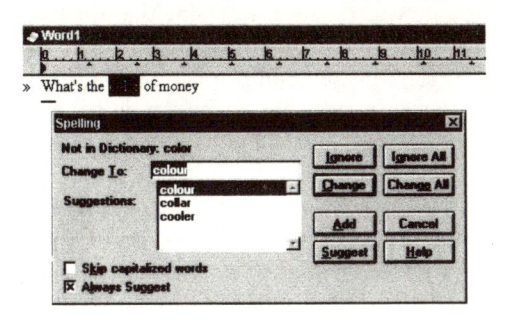

Fig. 40. Spellcheck dialogue box.

it comes to a word that is not in its dictionary, it stops and brings it to your attention. The dialogue box will give you some possible alternatives and it is then left up to you which choice you make.

- If the spelling is incorrect and you can see the correct spelling suggested, click on it and choose the appropriate command – this may be **Change, OK, Substitute** or **Replace**.

- If you know the spelling is correct, it may be that the dictionary doesn't hold that word. You can tell the checker to ignore and bypass this word without changing it. This normally applies to names, abbreviations or technical terms.

- If you know that the spelling is correct but it is a word that you know will crop up frequently, such as your town name, or your surname, you can then use the **Add** command. This adds the word to your dictionary. In future, every time it gets to that word it will be able to check its spelling.

- If the spelling is incorrect and none of the suggestions are correct, there is usually a space for you to type in the correct spelling, and then select change.

PREVIEWING AND PRINTING YOUR WORK

With a desktop publisher you can see on the screen what your page looks like – this is known as **WYSIWYG**, pronounced wizzywig, and stands for 'what you see is what you get'. With a word processor it is different. You cannot see the entire document that you have typed displayed on the screen, so you do not know exactly how it will look unless you use the **Print Preview** facility.

The print preview command can normally be found in the file menu; there may be a shortcut icon as well. This may have a picture of a piece of paper with a magnifying glass overlooking it, or maybe a picture of a printer inside a frame. Clicking on this shows you the full view of the piece of paper on your screen for you to check the layout.

Sending your instructions to the printer

If you click on the shortcut icon of a printer, this immediately sends a full copy of the current document to your printer. There are other options available if you choose **Print** via the file menu. This option will display a dialogue box that provides you with various choices, such as:

- How many copies do you wish to print?
- Do you wish to print all pages/odd pages/even pages?
- Do you wish to print a specific page/pages?
- Do you wish the pages to be collated, ie in order?
- Do you wish to print in colour or mono?
- Which printer do you want to send your work to?

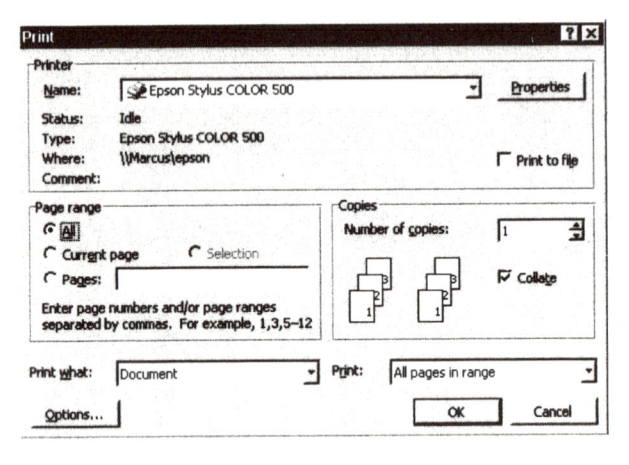

Fig. 41. Printer dialogue box.

Figure 41 shows how these questions are presented with an Epson printer. When you have made all your choices, click OK and your document will begin printing.

Looking at Programs for Correspondence

CASE STUDY

Beverly gets full marks

The teacher who heads the computer club has asked Beverly to prepare a *Programme of Events* for the school's open evening. She looks forward to putting her word processing and desktop publishing skills to good use.

- First she types in the main text for the programme of events.

- Next she uses the spellchecker to make sure she doesn't get an English detention.

- She then formats the work until she is happy with its appearance.

- To add interest she inserts a couple of cartoons and puts a copy of the school emblem on the front page.

When she presents it to her teacher the following week it is received with great enthusiasm and praise.

PRACTICAL EXERCISE

Now try a practical exercise on the word processor. Follow each step closely, but feel free to type in your own text instead of copying this example if you wish.

1. Open your word processor and select a new blank page. If this option isn't displayed when the program opens, then click on the word file to drop down the menu and click on new.

2. You will see a flashing cursor. This is where you begin typing.

3. Type in an address pressing the return/enter key after each line.

4. Press the enter key three times to create a space under the address.

5. Type in the date and press enter.

6. Now type in some text, either your own or copy two paragraphs from this book. Remember that you don't have to press the enter key at the end of each line, only at the end of the paragraph.

7. Now press the enter key a few times to create a space under the last paragraph and then type in your name.

This is where you can start to have fun:

1. Select your address by clicking and holding down the mouse cursor just in front of the first letter of the first line and then drag the mouse cursor along the line to the end. Notice how the text becomes highlighted as the cursor passes over it. Now, without releasing the mouse button, move the cursor down slowly and you will see that each line becomes highlighted. When the whole address is selected release the button on the mouse.
2. Now choose the icon for bold and click on it. You will see the writing expand to allow for the extra thickness in the letters. Now find the icon to centralise the text (Figure 36vi) and click on it. You will see the address jump to the centre of the page.
3. The last step is to make the address bigger. Choose the point size box and click on the little arrow at the side, which will give you a list of sizes available. Point to 18 and click on it. Now click your mouse cursor anywhere on the page to deselect the address text. You should now have your address in larger bold print in the centre of the page.

Don't worry if it seems to have gone wrong, just return to step 1 and try again. If all has gone well try some of the other options later.

Now cut out the first paragraph and paste it in after the second paragraph:

1. Following the procedure detailed above highlight the whole of the first paragraph.
2. Now click on the cut icon (Figure 36viii) or choose cut from the edit menu at the top of the page. Voila! The first paragraph has disappeared. Place your mouse cursor on the line following the end of the second paragraph and click.
3. Paste the first paragraph back onto the page by clicking your mouse cursor on the paste icon, or by selecting paste from the edit menu, and the lost paragraph will reappear in its new place.

Now you have completed this exercise try your own experiments. Try using each of the formatting techniques discussed in the chapter to change fonts, delete text, add words, etc. Experiment freely and remember if it does all go pear-shaped just click new on the file menu and start again.

11
Looking at Programs to Calculate With

Mathematical calculations are what computers were designed for, and programs such as spreadsheets and financial packages take full advantage of this, releasing you from the strain of working things out for yourself. A spreadsheet is a large grid comprised of boxes, known as **cells**, in which you enter your data. This data can appear in a cell as text or numbers. Numerical data can be shown in a variety of formats, eg date, currency or formulae. When set up correctly they will perform numerical and statistical calculations based on the data contained in the cells.

A financial package is already set up to perform these calculations. You just have to enter your banking and other financial details into the pre-constructed page layouts. These page layouts are simply a spreadsheet presented in a familiar way. All the calculations are performed automatically behind the scenes. Depending on the information entered, it will be possible to retrieve many different types of reports and graphs showing your true financial worth.

CALCULATING WITH SPREADSHEETS

The structure of a spreadsheet is made up of columns and rows forming boxes known as cells. Information that is entered into these cells can be in the form of text for headings and labels, numerical information, dates, times or formulae to perform calculations using data from other cells.

The initial screen of a spreadsheet has many similarities to a word processor. It has scroll bars, tool bars with icon shortcut buttons, menu selections and title bars. Many of the icons on the tool bar perform the same job as in a word processor – refer to the previous chapter for a description of each of these.

Identifying cells
- Each **column** is a line of cells going down the page – a letter at the top identifies the column.

- Each **row** is a line of cells going across the page – a number at the start identifies the row.

- The meeting point of the column and row is the **cell reference**. Cells are addressed by reference to the column and row, ie B4 as shown in Figure 42.

Fig. 42. Cell reference in spreadsheets.

A cell must be highlighted before information can be entered. Clicking the relevant cell with the mouse cursor will select it. A cell or a range of cells can be formatted to display information in a specific way. For example, the format may be set to display a number as currency, as shown in Figure 43. It will then automatically enter the pound sign and move the decimal point for two places so that the pence are displayed. Alternatively it may be formatted to show whole numbers only, in which case it will automatically round up or down accordingly. You have to tell the spreadsheet how you want it to interpret a cell's data by selecting the cell and choosing format from the menu selections.

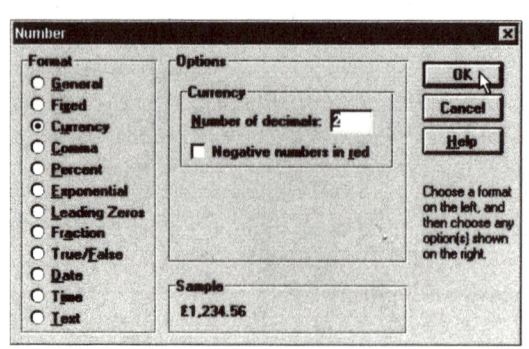

Fig. 43. Formatting number dialogue boxes.

Formatting the whole column or row

A complete row or column, or a designated area of cells, can be formatted as a group rather than one cell at a time. First the area has to be selected. Entire columns and rows can be selected by clicking

Looking at Programs to Calculate With

on their reference letter/number at the top or side of the sheet, as shown in Figure 44. Multiple cells can be selected by placing the cursor in the first cell of the desired area, holding down the mouse button and dragging the cursor over the required cells. Once an area is selected, the format menu can be chosen and whatever format chosen will be applied to the whole of the selected area, not just one cell. A selection of multiple cells is known as a **range**.

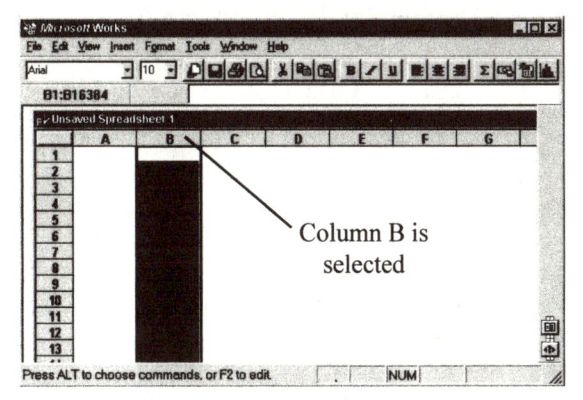

Fig. 44. A selected column.

Adjusting the width of columns/rows

The width of columns can be altered very easily in most spreadsheet packages. In Figure 45 the mouse cursor has been placed over the two lines that join columns F and G. It automatically changes into an **adjust** cursor: hold down the mouse button and drag left or right as necessary. The same method can be used for adjusting the height of rows. You will also find a facility in the menus whereby you can enter the size in figures, enabling greater accuracy when a number of rows/columns need to measure the same.

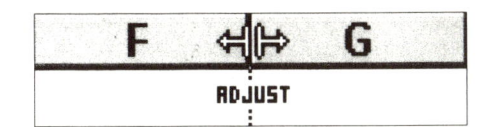

Fig. 45. The adjust cursor.

Entering the details

When entering text into a spreadsheet, it doesn't really matter whether you decide to format the style of the text first or later. However, when entering figures and dates, if the cell is formatted first it can save time and make your spreadsheet easier to follow as it grows. To show you an example of how the same entry can display differently depending on its cell format, do the following exercise. This is based on Microsoft Works but whatever package you have will work in a similar way.

1. Open up your spreadsheet package.

2. Select the second column B, choose format from the menu bar, click on **Number**.

3. Click on **Currency**. Format it to 2 decimal points, click OK.

4. Select the third column C and again choose format, number and currency.

5. This time, format it to 0 decimal points, click OK.

6. Nothing will have appeared to happen but the formatting has taken place, as you will now see.

7. On your spreadsheet in box A1 type 50. Do the same in B1 and C1.

8. They will be displayed as 50 (general format), £50.00 (currency to two decimal points), £50 (currency to no decimal points), as shown in Figure 46.

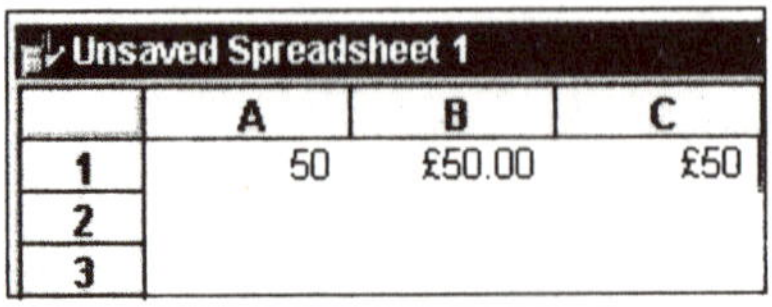

Unsaved Spreadsheet 1		
A	**B**	**C**
50	£50.00	£50

Fig. 46. Different format entries.

LETTING THE PROGRAM DO THE SUMS FOR YOU

Entering a formula into a cell instructs the system to perform calculations. The formula can consist of basic maths such as addition, subtraction, multiplication or division, to more complicated statistics such as averages, percentages and any other formula.

Looking at Programs to Calculate With 97

There are many pre-set **functions** available in spreadsheets that carry out particular processes. Each function has a name that the package recognises and understands.

Entering a simple formula

Before entering a formula, you need some information with which to perform a calculation. In the diagram showing a list of knives, forks, spoons and teaspoons (Figure 47), the total cutlery column is where the formula would be placed. If at any time a number is changed, the formula will automatically take this into account and display the revised total. In most spreadsheet packages a formula is entered in the following way.

	A	B	C	D	E	F
1		Knives	Forks	Spoons	T-Spoons	Cutlery
2	Drawer 1	15	20	50	30	115
3	Drawer 2	17	26	42	11	96

Fig. 47. Displaying calculation results.

1. Highlight the cell where the formula is to be placed. Type the 'equals' sign (=), this tells the system you want it to work out a calculation.

2. Next, you need to indicate which formula you wish to use by quoting its function name. In our example we need to add up the four sets of figures – the function name for that is **SUM**.

3. Then you need to state the area that the calculation applies to. In this example it is cells B2, C2, D2 and E2 – this can be entered as a range (**B2:E2**).

4. The formula entered into the cell F2 will resemble =**SUM(B2:E2)**.

5. An alternative way of entering it if you didn't know the function name would be = B2 + C2 + D2 + E2.

Just underneath the tool bar on most spreadsheets is a **command line**. This displays the information contained in the selected cell. A cell that has a formula entered will display the answer to that formula – to see the formula that is in the cell, select it and look at the command line. Cell contents can be edited on this command line by placing the mouse cursor where you wish to edit and clicking. In Figure 48 the first part shows which cell is selected, then there is a cross and a tick – these can be used to confirm your editing – finally there is the display of the cells' contents.

```
      F2            X ✓ =SUM(B2:E2)
```

Fig. 48. Displaying hidden formulae.

Using the cut/copy and paste commands

These commands can be used in much the same way as a word processor. Highlight the cell or range of cells with your mouse, click on the copy command from the edit menu, place the mouse cursor in the new position and select paste. If you are copying text, this will copy as expected. If you are copying anything other than text you have to be a little more aware of what you are copying and what might happen.

If you place a formula in a cell, the cell will display the result of that formula as shown in the diagram with the cutlery. However, if you copy that cell, it will copy the formula – not the answer. For example, if B2 = 15, C2 = 20, D2 = 50 and E2 = 30 then the formula in cell F2 (= SUM(B2:E2)) adds all these together – on your spreadsheet in cell F2 will be the answer 115.

If you then copy the cell F2 and paste it to cell F3, the formula will be copied but the range will adjust itself to the sum of B3 to E3 and display the answer to that – ie 96, as shown in Figure 47.

HOME ACCOUNTING WITH FINANCE PACKAGES

Accounting programs are an amalgamation of a spreadsheet and a database. The user sees familiar accounts to set up such as bank accounts, credit cards and loan accounts. The computer performs all the calculations automatically once the information has been fed into it.

A home finance package will keep an accurate running account of your financial details providing it is used correctly. It can be set up to track your regular income and expenditures and give a graphical representation of your financial status. For example, Figure 49 shows a page from a **Quicken** bank account. The entries are easy to understand and an accurate balance can be seen immediately.

Looking at Programs to Calculate With 99

As seen in the diagram, each transaction can be given a date, a type – such as cheque, direct debit, etc – a payee, an amount, a memo area for notes and a category. Categories are not compulsory, but if used the package will look at these details to analyse your spending habits. It can be quite an eye-opener if you've a strong stomach!

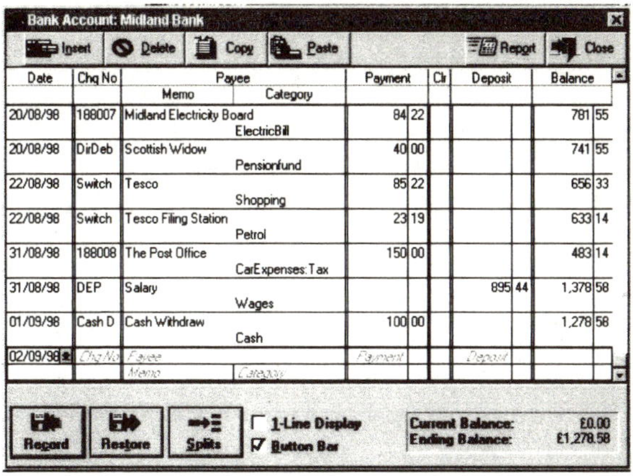

Fig. 49. A Quicken financial sheet.

How does it know my spending habits?
It is up to you to tell it. Once it knows, it will keep track of them and, unlike us, a computer never forgets about a payment that has to be made. The basic idea is like this:

- Set up a bank account that resembles your own. Tell the computer how much you have in there, not forgetting any transactions that have not yet been drawn.

- Create further accounts that mirror your savings, loan and credit card accounts.

- Every time you write a cheque or withdraw cash, etc remember to enter it into the relevant account.

- Find the area on your financial package that records regular payments such as direct debits. In Quicken it is under the **List** menu, called **Scheduled Transactions**. Enter all the details including which account the payment/receipt applies to, the date on which it occurs and the frequency, eg monthly.

- When you receive your statement use the **Reconcile** facility to match your records with the bank. Any errors will show up immediately.

BEING SHOWN YOUR SPENDING HABITS

If you allocate a category to each of your transactions, the package will be able to give a summary of your spending habits within each of these groups. For example, you could have categories including:

- income
- household bills
- house improvement
- food
- car expenses
- hobbies.

Each time you record a transaction, place it into one of these categories. After a period of time you will be able to obtain a report and see a graph of how much you have spent and on what, such as that shown in Figure 50.

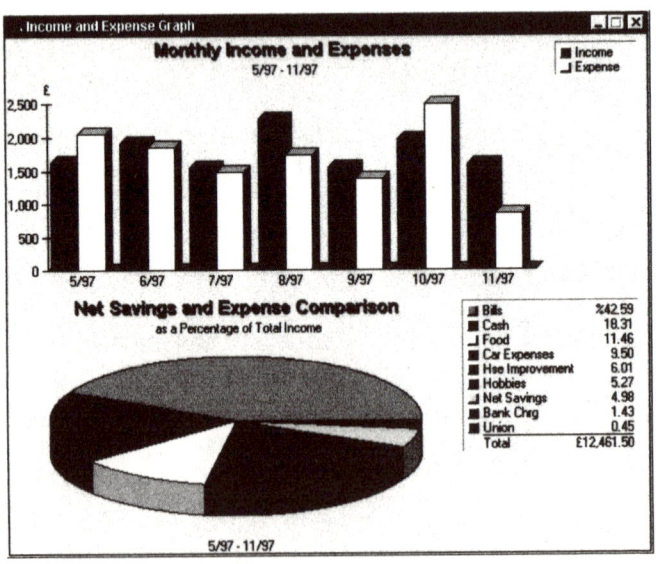

Fig. 50. Graphical representation of finances.

Looking at Programs to Calculate With

In Quicken you can use the categories area to transfer money from one account to another. For example, if you have a bank account called Midland and a credit card account called Visa, when you send a cheque to your credit card company, enter it from your Midland account in the usual way but in the category area select Visa. This will then also enter a credit transaction automatically into your Visa account, noting that you have paid some money off and adjusting the balance.

CASE STUDY

Mark does some work at home

As the sales manager for his firm, Mark is in charge of twelve representatives who form his sales team. He has recently had to reduce his team from fifteen and subsequently had to reorganise their areas to maintain national coverage. In order to monitor the efficiency of the new system he decides to use a spreadsheet to record the volume sales of each product for each member of the team.

He uses a separate column of the spreadsheet for each representative and the products are listed in rows. He adds a formula to work out the total value of each product sales and another to convert these figures into percentages of total sales. By keeping these figures updated regularly he can see at a glance how each sales area is performing, so that area boundaries can be amended if necessary to improve efficiency. He can also produce pie charts and graphs to present to his sales director at the beginning of each month.

PRACTICAL EXERCISE

Here you will learn how to use the **Fill Series** – this is automatic filling in of cells for certain data. It can save a lot of time in some areas. This example uses Microsoft Works version 4, but whichever package you are using will be very similar.

1. Select and fill in a cell with the word Sunday, click on the tick in the command line to confirm your entry.

2. Place your cursor over the cell again, click on the mouse button and hold it down while you drag over the next six cells to select them.

3. Your selection will be darker than the rest of the sheet, showing

it is highlighted, except for the first cell in the selection which has Sunday written in.

4. Click on the edit menu and select the command fill series. This will show a dialogue box with various options. It will be set to **AutoFill** – click on OK.

- Your highlighted selection will fill with the subsequent days of the week.

The fill series can be used for various other tasks such as filling in sequential numbers, dates, months, etc. Just highlight the area you wish to fill, remembering to include the first cell that you have written in so that the computer knows where to start. You can fill across the rows or down the columns – wherever you highlight.

12
Looking at Programs to Store Information

A program that stores information input by the user is called a **database**. You can think of it as a computerised filing cabinet, secretary and office junior all rolled into one – but without the tea-making facilities! It is a collection of information stored in such a way that it enables the user to perform reference and search tasks quickly and accurately.

As an example, suppose you wanted to create a database containing your video tape collection. In it you would give each video a number, describe the type of recording (series, film, documentary, etc), state the title or subject, give it a category (comedy, action, thriller, etc), maybe name the leading stars and the date that it was recorded. You could then, at any time, find out information such as:

- How many James Bond films you have in your collection.
- What comedy clips you have for when you need cheering up.
- How many videos you have in your entire collection to work out their value.
- Which films are available for that cosy night in with a glass of wine and a loved one.

Searches can be extended to more than one criterion, such as how many films you have starring Tom Cruise that were recorded more than two years ago. This way you get to watch one that you may have forgotten you had in your collection and that you haven't seen for a while. You may be wondering if it really is this simple, so let's have a look at how databases are built.

BUILDING AND USING DATABASES

A database is formed using three levels of ascending hierarchy:

1. The use of **Fields**. These store an individual item of information, eg the name of a film or the leading star.
2. A **Record**. This is the collection of all fields relating to the main item, eg all information relevant to one viewing.
3. The **File**. This is the collection of all records, eg the library of recordings.

The name of the file would usually resemble its contents, eg Videos. Figure 51 shows one record of a file containing the necessary fields.

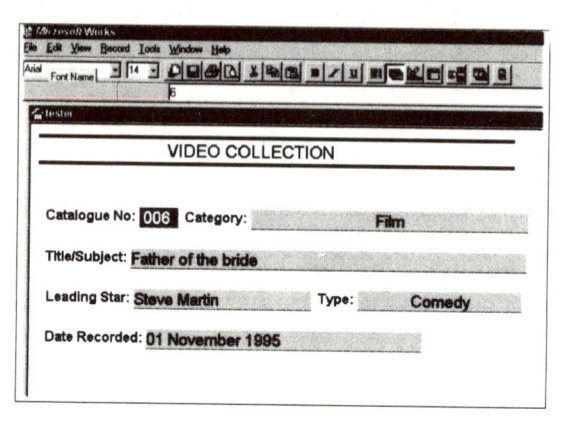

Fig. 51. A database record.

Building a database from scratch can be a challenging task. For those who want an easier route, programs usually contain a number of pre-formed databases that can be used just as they are, or adapted to your needs. They are called **templates**.

Choosing a template
Once a template has been chosen, some programs will modify them slightly for you by asking a series of questions. You may be asked how many fields you require in your record, you may be given the opportunity to name them and you may be offered various appearances to choose from such as **colourful**, **professional** or **informal** looking etc. All of these decisions can be changed later if they don't quite meet your needs.

Adapting a template
A database is designed to store and sort information for you – you just have to enter the information in the relevant places. You achieve

Looking at Programs to Store Information 105

this by each field having a **label**, which describes what type of information a field requires. Once the information is entered, the **tab** key on the keyboard is used to move on to the next field and so on, until all the information is entered for a complete record. You then move on to the next record and start again.

A template may not have the correct number of fields for your requirements and the sizes of them may need adjusting. Entering the **Design Mode** can easily do this. **Normal** use only allows you to enter information into the fields, design mode allows you to make changes to the field properties.

Once in design mode, programs may differ slightly as to how changes are made, but usually it is a case of double clicking on the relevant field to highlight it, then adjusting it accordingly. Some programs such as Microsoft Works have a protection feature that prevents you from accidentally altering any of the field labels. Once in design mode, look through the menu selections for the **Protection** command and disable it.

Label names can be changed, sizes of the fields can be adjusted to accommodate longer or shorter names, entry types can be formatted to accept only certain data such as numbers or dates, and the order of its selection can be amended.

Changing the entries

Changing the size of a field is often as easy as placing the mouse cursor over the edge of the field, holding down the mouse button and dragging it to the desired size, as shown in Figure 52. Moving a field from one place to another can be achieved in a similar way by placing the mouse cursor within the field and dragging.

Fig. 52. Enlarging a field.

What is tab order?

When using a database, starting at the top and working your way down, as you would complete a form, enters information. If you have adapted a template that involved moving the fields around, the order in which they will be selected when in normal mode may have been disrupted. Most databases will have a **Tab Order** command. This may be found either in the menu selections or within the properties box of the individual fields. Once you have finished the layout of your database, assign the correct tab number to each field in turn.

KNOWING WHAT DATABASES CAN BE USED FOR

There are many uses for databases. In the work environment they can be used to store information needed by the business such as customer names or invoice details. In the home environment they can be used to store names and addresses, recipes, music collections, book collections, inventories of household furniture, important account numbers – the list is endless.

Most environments use databases for statistical purposes. Every time you apply for credit you are probably entered onto a database somewhere – your payment record will then be monitored. When another company wishes to offer you credit they may check various databases for your credit status.

Using the search facilities

Databases usually have two ways to view the information stored in its file. These are often referred to as **form view** and **list view**. The first one shows a complete individual record in its entirety, as shown in Figure 51. Each record can be viewed in turn, using the record selector bar displayed on the screen as shown in Figure 53. It works by using the innermost arrows to move backwards and forwards through the file one record at a time. The outside arrows are short cuts, the left one takes you back to the first record and the right one to the last.

Fig. 53. Selecting records.

List view shows all records, enabling an overview of the complete file. This is most useful when you wish to search for particular pieces of information.

An icon on the tool bar, or a command in the menu selections called **Query** or **Search** will bring up a dialogue box where you can input the required information. You can tell the search to look at each individual field in all your records – which will be done in seconds – and present you with a list of any records that meet your requests. For example, as seen in Figure 54, you may wish to know from your video collection whether you have any documentaries on

Looking at Programs to Store Information 107

computers. You would need to tell the query to look in the category field and report any entries that are listed as documentaries *and* look in the title field to see if there are any entries containing computers.

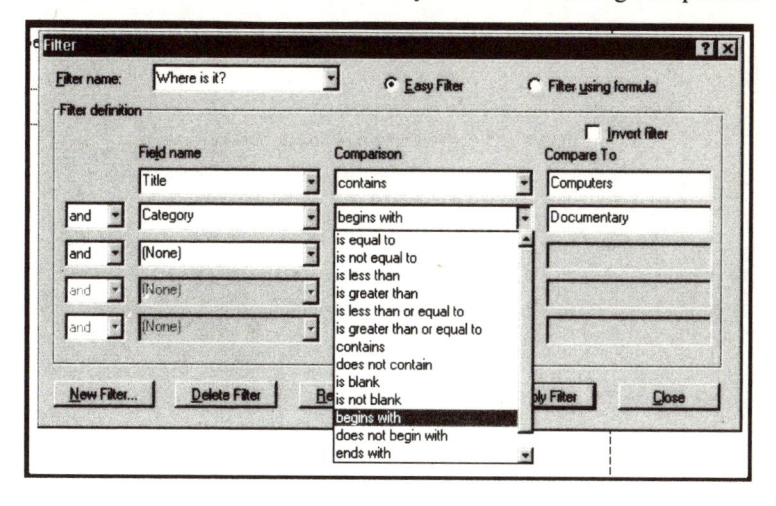

Fig. 54. Searching for information.

List view will then show all entries containing these parameters, enabling the desired recording to be selected. Because you chose the *and* feature as a further requirement, it will only list those documentaries that contain information on computers and not any other irrelevant documentaries.

KEEPING A DIARY WITH A PIM

A **PIM (personal information manager)** is a special type of database designed for ease of use. There is nothing to set up so you can start to use them straight away. As with all programs there are many to choose from, but the most common one included with a large number of new machines is the **Lotus Organiser**. This is available as part of the **Lotus SmartSuite** package or may be obtained as a stand-alone program.

Organiser resembles a normal Filofax-type diary and is used in exactly the same way. You can even hear the pages turning over! Entries are made using the **Create** option from the menu bar. Choose **Entry in** and you will be presented with a list of choices, one for each section of the diary. In Organiser you have the following sections for storing information.

- Calendar
- Things to do
- Addresses
- Calls
- Year planner
- A note pad
- An anniversary record.

Double clicking on any empty space in the organiser will also bring up a blank new entry form for the correct category.

You can have an organiser for each member of the family and you also have the facility to make your own customised organiser. For home use it is probably the only database you will want. Other features include:

- Regular appointments need only be entered once. Organiser will fill in the rest.

- You can set alarms to remind you of important events or calls.

- You can print out in many formats, including pages that can be inserted into regular Filofax-type diaries.

- You can link entries in different sections and move between them.

- Select an entry from the address book and it will dial the number for you and keep track of the time and cost of the call.

Most PIMs have similar features but you will need to use the on-line help to find ways to perform individual tasks.

CASE STUDY

Jean begins experimenting

Having grown more used to the computer Jean realises that the program she bought from the diet club is in fact a database. As she has found this program so useful, she decides to create a database for Eric's stamp collection.

She opens up the database program and selects to use a collection template. By using design mode she alters the titles of the fields to show the country, year, face value of the stamp and its cost. After entering all the details Eric can now find out easily how many of each

Looking at Programs to Store Information

stamp he has, how many from each country and the total value of his collection. He can also tell if he already has a particular stamp before making a purchase, without having to search through his albums.

PRACTICAL EXERCISE

As mentioned earlier in the chapter, you can format fields to enter only certain types of data. This exercise uses the Microsoft Works 4 program to show how to create a field that automatically numbers each record, and how to display a date in the same format on each record, regardless of how it is entered.

1. Open the Microsoft Works program, click on the works tools tab and select to create a new database.

2. In the dialogue box displayed, change the entry Field 1 to Video Number. This will be the label of your first field.

3. Click on the serialised button at the bottom of the list and change the starting number to 001. This tells the database you want it to number your records in this field.

4. Use the tab button to move to the increment area. Leave this at one, so that your records will increase in number each time by one, and click on add.

5. Amend Field 2 to Title of Video then click on add. This field can stay as a general entry.

6. Change Field 3 to Date Recorded, click on the date button and select an example of your chosen format, click add and then done.

7. Change to form view using the icon that looks like a stack of index cards – you should now be looking at your first record.

Now try your mini database
- The first field will not allow you to enter anything into it because this will be the number of the record.

- Tab to the title field and enter the title of a film.

- As you tab to the date field, the database will enter your first record number of 001.

- Type in a date in the following format – 11/6/98. Unless this is the format you chose to display your date, then as you tab to your next record the database will change the date to your chosen format.

- Fill in a few more records then flip back and forth through them to see how it builds up.

13
Looking at Programs for Having Fun

Very few people, despite all good intentions at the outset, resist the temptation to have a bit of fun with their computer – and why not? All work and no play, etc. The entertainment value of your computer should not be overlooked, indeed it should be exploited. Children, for instance, learn very well if they think they are playing. Let's look at how you can make use of this other side of the computing experience.

RELAXING AND LEARNING WITH GAMES AND EDUCATION

Games

There is a shattering array of games currently available to home computer users, with more hitting the shops all the time. Not all these are of the mindless violent type we have come to associate with the amusement arcade, and they can be split into classifications for a clearer view.

Simulations
These programs are designed to enable you to enjoy a specific experience from the comfort of your desk. They include such experiences as flying an aeroplane, driving a formula one car or managing a football team. Their emphasis is on realism, giving the user the feeling that they are actually doing it. These programs are not games in the sense that you have to achieve an end goal, but encourage escapism, such as success being the safe landing of a plane or a personal best lap time at Monaco.

It is fact that Jacques Villeneuve, 1997 World Formula 1 Champion, actually learned some racing circuits by playing a computer game and that pilots learn some manoeuvres on computer before trying the real thing. Yes, they are that real! The down side is that time can run away and late nights are the price you pay.

Strategy and adventure
These are the thinking person's computer game. Strategy and puzzles do not rely on speed and dexterity of the body but of the mind. Whilst they may not make the adrenaline flow they are certainly challenging and usually give the user a choice of difficulty settings. The player will be told what the objectives are and it will be necessary to solve puzzles and use some lateral thinking along the way. Some of these games can go on for months and cause a lot of frustration but are usually very satisfying to complete. You can involve the whole family trying to solve the problems you come across. They can be extremely addictive, so be warned!

Arcade and shoot-em-up
This section is usually where the blood-and-guts games fit in. Many games are not suitable for young children but the packaging should give a rating similar to those seen on videos. The reputation gives this category a bad name, but please be aware that many arcade games designed for young children involve good educational content. Recognising shapes, learning basic mathematics, spelling and elementary reasoning skills are used to full advantage in the better games. Children have to learn to use the keyboard, and recognise letters and numbers in order to play. With this as a carrot many children will learn their alphabet without the slightest idea that they are being taught it.

Old favourites
You can also purchase all the old favourite board games for use on the computer. Monopoly, Cluedo, Scrabble, card games and hundreds of others can be obtained, with many available as **shareware** for just a few pence. These take up very little room on the hard disk and are good for a few minutes' relaxation during the day.

Hopefully you won't abandon the thought of your computer as an item of entertainment, if you do you truly will miss out on a lot of its potential.

Education
This is probably the fastest growing section of mainstream programming. With the increasing numbers of computers in schools, and the inclusion of computer studies in the national curriculum, the production of educational software is big business. In addition to the educational arcade type programs mentioned earlier, specific subject programs are widely available. It is now

Looking at Programs for Having Fun 113

possible to buy programs teaching a wide range of GCSE subjects from beginners to exam level. The Open University also makes wide use of computer systems for learning.

With all these subjects an element of interaction is available. This means, for example, that the computer can set tests and mark your answers, or give you tutorials to follow involving questions and answers to check your progress. Many educational programs are multimedia, which gives the student the chance to see short video sequences or to hear a foreign language spoken. Biology programs will take you step-by-step through the human body, explaining each part and pronouncing difficult words.

ENCOURAGING YOUR CHILDREN TO USE REFERENCE PROGRAMS

Everyone who has children knows how difficult it is to encourage them to look things up in a reference book such as an encyclopaedia. With computerised reference material you will be surprised how that changes. Computerised encyclopaedias are very user-friendly multimedia programs, making their use easy for even the youngest child. They are packed with colour photographs, films, animations and text both written and spoken. **Encarta**, **Groliers** and **Encyclopaedia Britannica** are three of the most popular general reference guides available and all are multimedia.

An example of an item in an encyclopaedia

They work like this: If you wanted to look up some information on Africa, for instance, then you would be shown a map of the country with a brief text description. In the description you would see some words or phrases in a different colour; these are known as **links**. When you put your cursor over a link you will see it change to a hand. If you click on a link it will give you more detailed information on that particular subject.

In the above example you may see the word 'wildlife' appear in a different colour in the text. If you click on this you will be given a detailed description of the wildlife to be found, containing further links. If you see the word 'elephant' shown as a link then clicking on this may produce a detailed description of the elephant along with a short video film of them in their natural habitat. Links are a way of viewing related topics without the need to keep looking them up in an index. Figure 55 shows a typical multimedia reference screen.

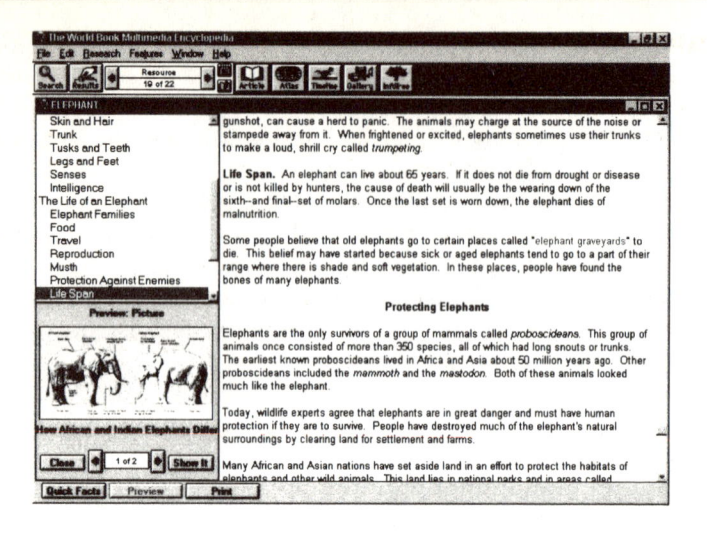

Fig. 55. Sample screenshot of an encyclopaedia.

Helping younger children too

Most reference programs also contain guided tours for younger children. These tours are spoken and the links are in the form of small pictures, enabling children too young to read to gain learning experience from them. You will be surprised just how fascinated youngsters from 1 to 100 will be. Learning has never been so much fun.

Using reference guides

There are also many more specific reference guides available for both home and professional use. Listed below are a few examples:

- drug names and uses (*Mimms*)
- the human body and how it works
- catalogues of various kinds, eg electronic components
- atlas and road maps
- cinema films
- the art world
- wines of the world.

And many hundreds of others covering almost any subject on earth. The cost of these programs varies from freebies to around £100 for the *Encyclopaedia Britannica*. Your computer will give you more information at your fingertips than turning your spare room into a library.

IMPROVING YOUR HOBBIES AND PASTIMES

Just as with the reference section above, virtually all hobbies and pastimes are available as programs for your computer. You may already have a hobby such as astrology, fishing or stamp collecting for which you can buy a program giving you tips, advice or reference. You may want to buy a program that will help you to keep records or help you build a family tree. They're out there somewhere.

It could be that you are thinking of taking up a hobby but want to be sure before spending lots of money. In this case just buy a program, put it on your computer and spend a few days looking through the information to see if it still appeals.

CASE STUDY

Lee improves his schoolwork

Mark and Lucy are concerned that Lee does not seem to be doing too well in mathematics at school. His teachers say he has plenty of ability but that it is difficult to stimulate his interest. That weekend they visit the local computer store and look through some educational software. They find a program that is suitable for Lee's age group and decide to purchase it. When they return home they install it on the computer and check it out. They find that it consists of a game in which a cartoon character has to be guided around a mathematical world rescuing numbers in order to complete various sums.

After two hours of checking it out they decide to see what Lee will make of it. He enjoys the game immensely and is totally unaware that he is in fact doing maths 'homework'. As the game has ten different levels of mathematical difficulty it will continue to be of benefit for some time to come.

SUMMARY

In this chapter you have looked at various types of programs that you can use to have fun and relax with. You can see that the computer has much to offer besides the more common uses of word processing, spreadsheets and other office based utilities. Your computer is a major investment and it will repay you well if you use it to its full advantage. It can be used to play games, learn new skills, assist you in your leisure pursuits and give you access to vast amounts of reference material. If you have children then the computer becomes an even more valuable tool, giving them the learning experiences that would have been impossible just a few years ago. Use it fully and above all enjoy it.

14
Communicating with the Outside World

A computer is, as you have seen, a very powerful and useful piece of equipment. It gives you the ability to perform tasks which were unimaginable a few short years ago. This is just the beginning. The computer now gives you the ability to travel the entire world in search of information using the Internet (information superhighway).

You have at your fingertips a machine which can:

- answer your phone
- send and receive faxes
- allow you to communicate in real time with people all around the globe for the price of a local phone call.

Your boundaries are truly your own imagination. Before looking in more detail at how to communicate with the help of a computer it is useful to define a couple of terms.

UNDERSTANDING THE TERMINOLOGY

What is e-mail?
E-mail is a form of written communication sent and received via the Internet. Documents sent this way are usually private because the recipient has to have a password to access them. It is sent as text and can be read as text at the other end, enabling alterations to be made and the document returned.

What is a fax?
A **fax (facsimile)** is sent using ordinary phone lines from one fax machine or computer directly to another. A fax is sent as a picture or graphic, and unless complicated and largely unreliable OCR (optical character recognition) software is employed, it cannot be altered or changed. As there is no control by the sender as to who picks up the fax at the other end, it should be regarded as an open letter and not confidential.

CONNECTING WITH A MODEM

Two things are required before you can use your computer to wander around the world.

1. A standard **telephone line**. As long as you have a phone in your house you don't need an extra line.

2. A **modem**.

What is a modem?

A modem is a card that can be fitted inside your computer in a spare expansion slot. It will have a socket on the back for you to plug in your ordinary phone and a cable with a plug on the end that fits into your telephone point. It is most convenient to have an extension socket fitted near your computer, or you can use a telephone extension lead obtainable from most good general stores.

A modem, short for modulator/demodulator, is a device for converting computer data signals into audio signals that can be transmitted along normal phone lines. There must also be a modem at the other end to convert the signals back again for the receiving computer. Modems can also be fitted externally to a computer via the serial port.

Once the modem has been fitted it will need to be configured for your system. Different makes of modem have different configuration routines, but you should have clear instructions in the box and the whole job will take you about an hour. Windows 95 and 98 users will be pleased to know that they can install their modem using the **add new hardware** routine found in control panel. With this method Windows will ensure you avoid conflicts with your other devices.

SETTING UP A FAX/ANSWERING MACHINE

Most modems these days are capable of handling faxes. If yours is of this type, it will have set itself up during installation. The easiest way to send a fax is through your word processor. Once you have typed it out, select print from the file menu. Change the setting from printing to your usual printer, to printing to the fax driver – this will begin the fax wizard where you can enter the phone number details. Microsoft Fax, which used to be bundled with Windows 95, allowed you to send faxes independently of a word processor, but this has been left out of Windows 98. Unlike a dedicated fax machine your computer will store faxes received as a file on your hard disk for you to view at a convenient time rather than print them out. If you then want to print them of course you can.

Most new **fax/voice modems** will come with a software package such as **Supervoice** that will enable you to set your computer up as a complete telephone exchange. You may wish to connect a microphone to your sound card in order to record your message and these can be purchased for under £10 from any electrical or computer store. Alternatively you can use the handset of your telephone. Once set up your computer will:

- Answer the phone and determine whether it is a fax or voice message coming in.
- If it is a fax it will store it for you to look at later.
- If it does not hear a fax tone it will assume the caller is human and play them your message.
- When the caller leaves a message it will be stored on your hard disk as a sound file ready for you to listen to later.
- You can also store documents for others to retrieve from your computer via their fax machine or computer.

Programs such as Supervoice will come ready configured as a simple answering machine – all you need to do is install the program. Your computer needs to be left on and the program open in order for it to work. If you are going to be using your computer then it can be minimised on the tool bar.

E-MAIL AND THE INTERNET

E-mail is probably one of today's biggest computer and business buzzwords. In this section you will see what it is and how you can get involved.

When you send a letter to somebody:

- You write the body of the letter then put it in an envelope.
- On the envelope you put the address of the person to whom you are sending it, and a stamp.
- You put the envelope in the postbox and, hopefully, a day or so later it arrives at its destination.

With e-mail (short for electronic mail) you:

- Type your letter on the computer.
- Enter the recipient's e-mail address in the box.
- Click on send and within seconds it is delivered.

This means that, providing the recipient is at the other end, you can have your reply in a couple of minutes – instead of a week. You can also attach files to be sent with your mail, eg a voice message or a photo.

One big advantage is cost. To send an e-mail letter costs the price of a local phone call. If you send several letters at cheap rate phone times you would send them all for a total cost of around 1p. So how does it all work? The answer is the Internet.

What is the Internet?
The Internet is a network of thousands of dedicated computers worldwide. Each computer is linked to several others via ultra high speed digital telephone lines. You send your message to one of these computers via your modem, and that computer then looks at the address and forwards it on. This is a great simplification of the real journey your message may in fact take. As explained earlier, each computer on the net is linked to several others but not all of them. Your message may in fact have to be transmitted to America then Japan, before finally ending up via Germany at its address in Paris. The net will use whichever route is currently the quickest, it will still take less than a minute and you won't even be aware of it!

How is it possible for me to send e-mail?
You cannot send e-mail straight from your computer to its destination because you need access to the Internet, and unless you have the odd few thousand pounds for a dedicated high-speed line, you first have to send it to someone who does. This is called an **Internet Service Provider** (**ISP**). The first step is to sign up with an ISP such as **CompuServe**, **AOL** or **Demon**. Prices will vary according to the services provided but will be no more than £10 per month. There are a few companies offering ongoing free connection now, so all you pay is the cost of your phone calls. Many computer magazines will have trial versions attached to their cover and this is an ideal way to find the one that suits you best.

Once you are registered with your chosen ISP you will be given your e-mail address and be ready to go.

- Begin by opening your ISP program.
- From the menu at the top of the page select E-mail.
- Choose Compose New E-mail.
- Enter the address you wish to send to.
- Type your message and click on the Send Now button as shown in Figure 56.
- Congratulations! you have sent your first e-mail.

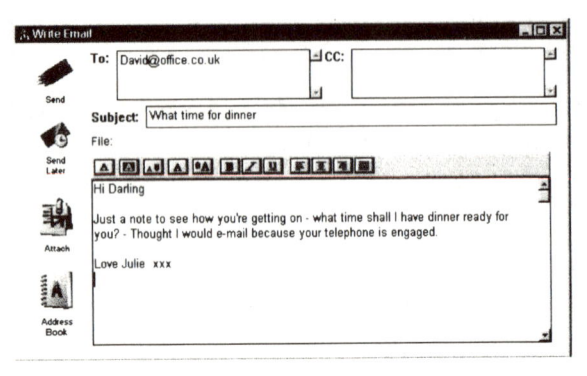

Fig. 56. An e-mail being written.

If you receive any e-mail messages then they will be held by your ISP in your mailbox. Next time you **log on** you will be informed that you have post and can either read them or print them out.

Saving money!
Exercise a little caution to save your phone bills from mounting up. You do not have to log on to the ISP to type your e-mail. You can save money by composing it **off-line**, meaning without being connected, and sending it later. With AOL you can set up what is known as a **flash session**. This enables you to set a time when your e-mail is to be sent and received. You can then compose all your e-mail and leave the ISP program running but do not log on. When the time comes along for your flash session the computer will log on for you and only stay on line long enough to send your mail and download any that you have received. You can then read your mail at your leisure or print it off without incurring charges.

WANDERING AROUND ON THE WORLD WIDE WEB

You learned in the previous section that the Internet is comprised of many computers linked to many others – but not to all. This process is known as **Webbing** and it is this that gave birth to the term **World**

Wide Web (WWW). You will often see these letters included in the address line of a Web site. Most ISPs will provide you with your very own Web site, which is like a notice-board where you can place adverts or whatever for others to see. You will see many adverts that invite you to 'visit our Web site at WWW, etc'. If you take them up you will see the sort of things that can be placed there with a little imagination!

Surfing the net

The process of looking around on the Internet is known as **surfing the net**. This can be great fun but watch your phone bill! Most sites that you visit will allow you to copy files, pictures or even whole programs to your computer to use when you are off-line. This process is known as **downloading**. It is this process that will run up your phone bill if you're not careful. Downloading a program could take from a few minutes to several hours, depending on its size, although it will normally give you an indication as to how long it is likely to take. Another point to remember is that while you are logged on to the net your phone is in use and callers will be unable to get through to you.

Using a browser

Your ISP will have what is known as a **browser**, which will normally start up when you log on. This will give you access to many features of the Web instantly, for example travel information, news, weather reports or what's showing at every cinema in the country. Figure 57 shows an example of the AOL browser.

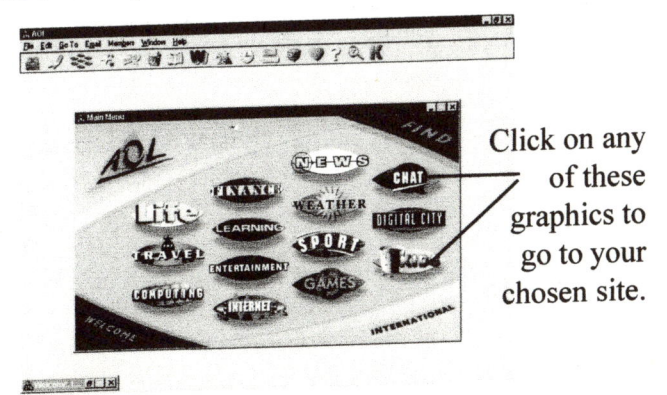

Fig. 57. The AOL browser.

You can find just about anything on the Web such as:

- the latest pictures from Mars, by hooking into the NASA computers
- a pen pal in any country you choose
- clips from the latest movies
- a way to talk to your latest pop idol.

The list is just about endless.

Finding what you're looking for

The term **search engine** is one that you are likely to come across in your adventure and you will be using it constantly without knowing it. A search engine is a very powerful program which enables you to enter a key word or phrase that you want to look for information on. Once you have entered your key word the search engine chugs away looking for references to it in its huge databases, then displays the results for you to see. When you see a site that you think may hold the information you want, click on it and the address will be contacted for you.

How to avoid seeing what you don't wish to see!

Inevitably with something as huge and as publicly accessible as the net, there will be things on it that you would not want to see or want your children to see. For this reason your ISP will provide the subscriber with a utility called **Parental Control**. Most offensive materials are accessed via newsgroups. Parental controls enable you to prevent access to those you deem unsuitable. ISPs are keen to keep you happy with their service so if you need specific help don't hesitate to contact them. The Internet itself cannot be policed or censored, as there is no single body in control of it. It is essentially too big to be controlled.

Having the resources of the entire world at your fingertips is, for many of us, too big a concept to come to terms with quickly. The only way to find out if it will benefit you is to try it. Have fun and don't be afraid to wander, after all at off peak times it is only costing you a penny a minute so you can have nearly half an hour for the cost of a stamp! Don't forget to use the free trial offers for ISPs.

CASE STUDY

Mark and Lucy go on-line

Now that they are familiar with their computer Mark and Lucy decide to register with an Internet Service Provider. They use a cover

Communicating with the Outside World

disk from their latest computer magazine, which entitles them to forty hours free access to try it out.

Lucy wastes no time in accessing the Open University to see what is on offer. She is amazed at the information and help that is available to her. She also finds that there is an on-line chat room in which students can communicate with each other, exchanging views and giving help and support. A chat room is an Internet site you can access that gives you the opportunity of communicating with others in real time. This means that when you type something on your keyboard and press the enter key, it appears on the screen of everybody else who is also logged on to that site. This enables free-flowing written conversations to take place between any number of people. There are hundreds of chat rooms covering all topics.

Lee and Beverly want to use the net to find a pen friend in a different country. Beverly decides that as she lives in Stratford-on-Avon UK she would like to write to someone in Stratford-on-Avon in America. She logs on to the Internet and looks at the ISP membership list for her chosen town. She then selects one of the e-mail addresses shown and writes a short letter of introduction. The following night when she logs on she finds that she has received a reply and has made a new friend.

PRACTICAL EXERCISE

For this exercise you will go to America and look at the government NASA space centre to see what is on offer. Don't panic, remember it is all for the price of a local call!

1. Open your ISP program, eg AOL.

2. Choose the option for direct access to the Web.

3. You will see an address line at the top of the page. In this box type the address hyperlink **http://www.nasa.gov/** Remember there are no spaces and it must be exactly as shown. The first part of the address http:// may already be there so don't type it again, just add the second part with no spaces.

4. Press the enter key and you will connected with NASA!

5. You can now choose any further information from the links on this page.

It really is that easy. Now try using the **Find** command to search for another site.

15
Finding Even More Practical Uses

Throughout the book you have looked at many uses of the computer system and the benefits that they bring. This final chapter looks at a couple of additions to your system that will add to its flexibility and further enhance its abilities.

ADDING PICTURES WITH SCANNERS

At some time or another all computer users will wish to add pictures to their work. Many pictures are readily available as clipart on disk as discussed earlier, but what if you cannot find the picture you want or you specifically need to use one of your own, for example a photograph of your house or yourself? The answer is to purchase a scanner.

A scanner is a device like those incorporated in photocopiers. In fact a photocopier is basically a scanner and laser printer built into one box. It works by passing a light source across the image, reducing it to a series of very small dots that the computer can store in memory. The number of dots that the image is broken down into is called the **resolution** – the more dots the higher the resolution. This means of course that the higher the resolution an image is scanned at, the more memory the computer needs available to store it.

There are many different scanners available, but they fall mainly into three categories:

- **hand held scanners**
- **page scanners**
- **flatbed scanners.**

Which scanner you choose depends not necessarily on how much you want to spend, but on what type of work you wish to scan.

Using hand held scanners

This type of scanner is only suitable for scanning small items. They look, at first glance, similar to a rather large mouse and are held in the hand in the same way. You line up the guide with the image you wish to scan and click the start button. You will see the light at the front of the scanner. The scanner is then slowly dragged across the image to copy it into the computer. When you have finished simply click the stop button, or the start button again, and hey presto the image is now stored on your computer.

This group is the cheapest form of scanner, with prices ranging from around £20. This does not mean that the results are not as good as the more expensive types, far from it. Hand held scanners produce pictures of superb quality from simple line diagrams to full colour photographs.

These scanners are most useful when copying an image from a book -- when you don't want to rip out the page. It is also particularly useful when you just want to copy a small part of a page, as the memory requirements will be much less. Their main drawback is that they are limited to a scan of about four inches wide. This is an obvious handicap if you want to copy a whole sheet of A4 size paper. It is possible to accomplish this by making two scans and **stitching** them together using software designed for the purpose. This software will usually be included free with the scanner, although if you are using a good quality image-editing package then they will have a routine included for doing this.

If you intend doing a lot of scanning involving whole page images and photographs, then you should consider purchasing one of the other types.

Using page scanners
As their name suggests these will scan a complete page, although software is available that will enable you to choose a specific area if you wish. Some page scanners are just larger versions of the hand held ones mentioned in the previous section, although most will have automatic facilities.

With automatic scanning, the page you wish to copy is placed at one end of the scanner and fed through automatically at the correct speed to produce the best result. One of the biggest benefits of this is that you don't get any hand twitching distortion in the final image. You will be surprised at how difficult it is to keep your hand steady for even the short time necessary for the scan with a hand held one. If you don't have auto-scan, then use a rigid guide such as a ruler to keep the image straight.

Using flat bed scanners

This group of scanners is probably the most versatile of all and for general home use will prove more than adequate. They look and operate much like a photocopier. You lift up the lid and place your document on the glass, close the lid and press a button. They are all automatic and very simple to operate, but like a photocopier are sometimes difficult when it comes to scanning a page from a book or magazine because of the thickness. Prices for this group start at around £50.

Once the image has been scanned into your computer you can use it like any other piece of clipart. You can alter it, add titles to it or manipulate it in any one of a thousand ways. It can be great fun editing your holiday snaps or re-touching them before printing them out, such as removing red-eye or putting Auntie Jean's head on Uncle Ben's body! Using your imagination you will enjoy yourself no end.

MAKING MUSIC

The computer perhaps does not rank very high on people's list of their favourite musical instruments. The truth is that many contemporary musicians write, arrange, edit and in some cases record their work solely with the use of a computer. How is this possible?

Most of today's computers will have a sound card fitted to them. At the rear of the system unit will be holes to plug in speakers and microphones. There is another socket for a 15-pin plug to be inserted. This socket is usually used to plug in games controllers such as **joysticks**, but it does have another use. It is also the sound card's **MIDI (Musical Instrument Digital Interface)** port through which your computer can communicate with electronic musical instruments such as keyboards and synthesisers.

Modern electronic musical keyboards are designed with the computer very much in mind. On the more expensive models there will be a floppy disk drive that accepts disks from the computer. This means that music can be composed on the computer and saved to disk, this disk is then inserted into the keyboard and the music played back. If you ever wondered just how one man with a keyboard can sound like a whole group then look no further. Many solo musicians will record onto disk the entire backing track necessary for each of their numbers. Once on stage they can then concentrate on their solo instrument part and vocals. It's a little like professional karaoke and not regarded as cheating. In theory you could do a whole show without being able to play at all, although that *is* regarded as cheating!

Becoming a home composer

The software required for becoming a home composer can range from simple shareware programs to full professional packages costing hundreds of pounds with full studio mixing desks. Most of the medium price range programs, £30 and up, will allow you to compose and edit music for several instruments. This will appear on the page as a single score with a separate stave for each instrument. You then place the various notes on each stave and when satisfied you can ask the computer to play the whole score or each stave. By utilising the chips built into your sound card, most reasonable music packages will be able to reproduce the sound of around a hundred musical instruments in much the same way as a keyboard. You will also be able to print the completed score or each instrument's part separately.

Unfortunately the one thing a computer can't substitute for or replace is a tone-deaf ear and a total lack of musical ability. If you do know even just a little then you will undoubtedly be able to improve and build on your skills with your computer's help.

UPGRADING YOUR COMPUTER

Most computer owners fight shy of removing the lid and touching anything inside it. This is good news for computer engineers and stores but bad news for the wallet. Most computer upgrades can in fact be carried out at home in just a few minutes with the use of a screwdriver and a little common sense. The following are the more important rules to obey when working inside the box.

- Always make sure you turn it off at the mains and unplug it.

- Never be tempted to work inside the computer when it is still turned on.

- Always handle components by their edges, as static electricity will destroy them.

- Wear an earth strap attached to your bare wrist – these cost only a pound or two and will prevent static from accidentally damaging components.

- Have a pen and paper ready to write down which wires go where and which way round cables are attached – if necessary write on the cables with a felt-tip pen.

128 Managing Your First Computer

- *Never* try to repair or open a power supply – they contain capacitors that can hold a lethal charge for some time after the computer has been turned off. We once saw a power supply that had the following label stuck on and have never forgotten it, 'If you try to mess with me – I will do my best to kill you'.

- If in doubt, do nowt.

- Don't try to repair monitors unless you know what you are doing.

Deciding if you can do it yourself

Common upgrades that can easily be carried out at home
- adding more memory
- adding a modem
- adding a scanner
- upgrading your sound card or video card.

Slightly more technical but still possible upgrades
- fitting a larger hard drive
- installing a CD-ROM
- upgrading to a better processor.

Best to call an engineer type upgrades
- changing a motherboard
- changing a power supply.

Making checks

Remember to always follow the instructions that come with your product, and when making a purchase check to make sure it will be compatible with the hardware you already have. If you own a Pentium computer you may have two different kinds of memory, SIMM (single inline memory module) 72-pin or DIMM (dual inline memory module) 168-pin. If upgrading using SIMMs they must be fitted in pairs, whereas DIMMs can be fitted singly. DIMMs and SIMMs should not be mixed, although it has been known to work.

CASE STUDY

Eric purchases a scanner

Eric has found his database on stamp collecting really useful but has decided it would be nice to be able to see a picture of the stamp when he looks it up. He decides to purchase a hand scanner so that he can add these pictures into his database.

Fitting the scanner is simply a question of taking out the four screws holding on the top of the system and inserting the scanner card into an empty expansion slot. The whole job takes him less than fifteen minutes. He then installs the software that came with the scanner, following the instructions on the screen.

Within half an hour of starting he is happily scanning in pictures of his favourite stamps straight out of the album. He stores his pictures in a directory called clipart using a subdirectory called stamps. In this way he will always know exactly where they are and can easily back them up onto a floppy disk to keep them secure.

His final task is to alter the database by adding a picture field in design mode.

Appendix
Suggested System Requirements

Knowing what computer system to buy to meet your needs can be confusing enough for those who understand computers. If you don't know anything about them it can be a nightmare. In this section you will find some suggested requirements to perform a variety of tasks. First a brief description of some of the terms you will come across.

KNOWING THE TERMINOLOGY

RAM (random access memory)
This is the everyday working memory installed in a computer – do not confuse it with the hard disk size, which is also measured in megabytes. The more megabytes you have, the more data the system can load into it from the hard disk when you call up a program for use. This generally means that the system will work quicker. Sixteen megabytes (Meg) of memory will be sufficient for an older computer running DOS and Windows 3.11. Systems with later Windows versions will run on 16 meg but you should consider 32 meg to be the minimum – 64 meg or more would be even better.

As a rule of thumb you should buy the most memory you can afford – many new software packages will not run effectively with less than 32 Meg.

CPU (central processing unit)
This is the brain of the system. Older computers with a 386 or 486 processor will be suitable for very basic computer requirements although these machines are now obsolete. The lower end Pentium or equivalent type processors provide better power. Though these are still not fast enough for most modern games, they may be a good buy second hand as a starter machine. Later processors include the MMX instruction sets for multimedia applications. Examples are the Pentium II, AMD K26, the Celeron and the IBM/Cyrix 6x86.

Processor speed (MHz)
This is measured in megahertz (MHz) and descriptions such as 350

Appendix

Pentium indicate a Pentium processor running at 350 MHz. The higher the number the faster the speed of the system. This could be compared to car engines – the low end 1100s would be the older 120/133 MHz, middle of the spectrum 1300/1500s would be the 233/266s and the fast 2.8litre would be the 450MHz.

Graphics card
This is a term used to describe the electronic circuitry that generates the picture for the screen. These cards also have memory fitted to them exclusively for use by the card. If you intend to do a lot of graphic work, or to play modern games that have a lot of complicated graphics built into them, you will want a card with at least eight Meg of graphic memory and the ability to render 3D effects. This type of card is known as a **3D accelerator card**.

Secondary cache
Memory is used by the processor to anticipate what actions you may do next. There is no need to say any more about this except that on a new system, you should be looking for 512kb supplied.

CD-ROM drive
These are advertised by their speed. Sixteen speed is the very minimum requirement and you will probably find 32 speed more usually specified. Again opt for the fastest you can.

Modem
These are also sold on speed. The slowest you should get runs at 33kbds but the faster 56kbds models are a better buy. The number of pieces of information that can be transmitted in a second defines speed in this instance. If you are intending to use the Internet then the faster speeds will save you money as it will send and receive at a substantially faster rate.

Hard disk size
This is also described in megabytes, which leads to confusion amongst newcomers. The megabytes on a hard disk are not memory – they are storage capacities, and are not related. Megabyte is merely a unit of measurement, 8 bits equal 1 byte and this is the amount of space required to store one character. Thus 1 megabyte will store one million characters. Hard disks have now increased in size to the extent that they are more commonly described in **gigabytes**, which is 1,000 megabytes.

A 4 gigabyte hard drive will store a lot of programs, but if you are intending to have a look at a few of the modern games on the shelves these days, then consider a bigger size. Perhaps six gigabytes or more would be reasonable, because those games soon eat up the space!

Monitors

These come in a variety of sizes with the standard now being 15ins. Having a bigger screen does not necessarily make everything displayed on it bigger. The benefit of a larger screen is that you can run most programs at a higher resolution and thereby displaying more information on it. If you try to display too much information on a smaller monitor you will strain your eyes trying to read it.

PUTTING IT ALL TOGETHER

The following puts these terms into perspective and gives a few examples of what system may be suitable for a given set of requirements.

Example 1

Margaret is a student and has no particular interest in computers. She does, however, recognise the fact that she could make good use of one for preparing her work and printing it out for submission. She will not be using graphics and will not want to play games.

Requirements
Almost any computer would suffice in Margaret's example. A secondhand 166 computer with 16 megabytes of ram and a hard disk of between 1 and 3 gigabytes of storage would allow her a degree of flexibility later, just in case. A modem can also be fitted if required. In order to print out her work she will need a small inkjet printer.

Example 2

John is a design engineer and wishes to use a computer to run a CAD (computer aided design) program. He will not be playing games as the computer is for business only.

Requirements
Modern CAD programs benefit from a fast computer with plenty of ram and a good graphics standard. He would be best to purchase a machine with a processor speed of at least 400 MHz. He will also benefit from having 128 Meg of ram and an eight Meg graphics card. CAD files can generate very large files so a hard disk with a

capacity of 11 gigabytes would be good. John also has to purchase a special type of printer known as a **Plotter**. This type of printer uses pens to draw lines on paper and is used particularly by engineers and architects. These printers cannot reproduce picture-type graphics, as they are limited to line work.

Example 3
Mary and Richard want a home computer for general family use. Their children will want to play games and they will use the Internet to keep in contact with members of the family in America.

Requirements
They will need to buy a multimedia computer system with an up-to-date specification. A typical example would be a Pentium II 350 with 64 Meg of ram and hard disk between 4 and 8 gigabytes. The CD-ROM drive would have a speed of 32x and a graphics card of 4 or 8 Meg. A 56k modem would round the package off nicely. They should also get a sound card and a decent set of speakers. The games would require a joystick and a colour printer would be necessary to be able to derive full benefit from the system.

Example 4
Colin and Pat would like to learn about computers but do not wish to get involved with the Internet. Their budget is limited, they would rather purchase a machine that could grow with them as they learn.

Requirements
It would be best for Colin and Pat to purchase a modern machine so that the possibility of upgrading in the future is open to them. A low-end processor such as the Celeron 233-300 MHz will ensure a modern motherboard that could take a faster chip in the future. They could start off with 32 Meg of ram and a 2 gigabyte hard drive – although this may limit them if they try out some of the modern games, they can always increase these at a later date. A 24 speed CD-ROM will again suffice with a run-of-the-mill 16 bit sound card and speakers.

With the above specification, a 4 megabyte graphics card and a 15in screen would finish the package off nicely. In the early part of 1999, this type of system was advertised for less than £500!

Glossary

Application. A program that performs a practical task, examples are a word processor and desktop publisher.

Backslash. The key usually found in the bottom left-hand corner of your keyboard. Separates directories, sub-directories and files in the path command.

Backup. A further copy of a program or file in case the original is lost or damaged.

Boot up. Simply means turning the computer on.

Browser. A graphic user interface used when logged onto the Internet, making it easier to find information.

Bulletin board. An electronic notice-board accessed via the telephone network. They also provide other services to subscribers, such as access to the Internet or addresses for e-mail.

Byte. Eight 'bits' make a 'byte'. One byte is the size of memory required to hold one character.

Cells. Small boxes in a spreadsheet in which information is put.

Clipart. Pictures or graphics that can be used in computer programs.

Control panel. An area within the Windows program that enables the user to perform various tasks such as changing the settings of their colour scheme, adding a printer, etc.

CPU (central processor unit). The brain of the computer where all the hard work is done.

Crash. This happens when a computer gets confused and stops responding to your instructions. The usual method of recovery is to switch off the machine, wait 20 seconds and switch back on again. This method will usually clear the confusion.

Cursor. The flashing bar that indicates where the next thing you type will appear, or the arrowhead if you are working in Windows.

Data. Information fed into the computer.

Database. A program that stores information, eg customer records, in a filing system that allows various ways of retrieving the same information, eg by customer name, invoice number, etc.

Glossary

Desktop display properties. A dialogue box that enables the user to change the appearance of the display on the screen.

Destination drive. The drive to which files are to be copied or saved.

Disk. An item for storing computer information. This can be in the form of a hard disk inside the computer, or the portable kind such as floppy disks and compact disks.

Disk space. The area available on the relevant disk for storing information on. Not to be confused with memory.

Document window. A display area on the front of the screen that enables the user to view the document. This will usually be in addition to the program window that will sit behind.

DOS. An operating system comprising programs that enable the user and the computer to understand each other and carry out instructions by typing in commands.

Dot matrix. An inexpensive type of printer that produces copies by its pins hitting against an ink ribbon.

Download. A term used on the Internet meaning to transfer documents, files or programs from the relevant place on the Internet to your own computer for personal use.

DPI (dots per inch). This defines the resolution that an image is printed at – the higher the DPI number, the finer the finished image.

Drives. The various devices available in a computer to read and write information from and to.

Drop-down menu. These appear automatically when you select a menu heading from the menu bar in a program. They literally drop down from the menu heading. Pop-up menus are the same but in reverse.

E-mail. A way of sending messages from computer to computer across a network, to be left in a person's e-mail letter box.

Expansion slots. Slots on the motherboard of a computer that enable the fitting of expansion cards to increase the capabilities of the system.

FAT (file allocation table). The index system a computer creates at the very beginning of a disk to enable it to locate all files stored on that disk.

File. The way computers store and save information or data so that it can be retrieved and used at a later date.

Flash session. A term used by AOL (America On-line) that enables the user to compose e-mail without connecting to the Internet, thereby saving money. A flash session can be activated that has the effect of connecting, sending written e-mail and receiving new e-mail then disconnecting.

Floppy drive. A device that allows a floppy disk to be read or written to by the computer. Often referred to as the A:\ drive.

Folder. Windows 95 term for a directory. An individual area where files are stored.

Font. A set of characters made up from letters of the alphabet, numbers and symbols that are all of the same style.

Format. This term has two meanings. 1. Formatting when referring to a disk, means to prepare it to receive data and/or to wipe clean a previously used disk. 2. Formatting when referring to text means to edit and change the layout until it looks the way you want it to.

Gigabyte. 1,000 megabytes. Used to measure the storage size of hard disks.

Graphic user interface. A program such as Windows that uses pictures and diagrams for you to point at and click with a mouse instead of using the keyboard – making the using of a computer far more user friendly.

Hard copy. Copies of files that are output via the printer.

Hard disk. The mass storage area inside the computer on which programs and data are stored.

Inkjet. A mid-range type of printer that produces copies by spraying ink onto the paper.

Input. The entering of data into a computer.

Interface. Something that allows one component of a computer to communicate with another.

Internet. A worldwide network system of computers to which anyone with a modem and the appropriate software can connect.

ISP (Internet service provider). A company that provides computer users with access to the Internet.

Joystick. A device that enables greater control when playing games or using simulators.

Justify. A term used in the formatting of text, referring to the alignment of lines.

Keyboard. This plugs into the computer and enables input by use of pressing various keys.

Landscape. A term for a piece of paper turned sideways so that it is wider than it is tall. Also known as wide.

Maximise. Enlarging the view of a window to fill the screen.

Megabytes (meg). The size of memory. One megabyte equals 1,048,576 bytes.

Memory. Special chips used to hold information for processing.

Glossary

Menu. A list of commands that perform various tasks on the selected area or object when clicked on with the mouse pointer.

Merging. The process of joining information from different documents.

Minimise. To temporarily remove a program or document from full view. Minimising reduces the view to an icon at the bottom of the screen or task bar.

Modem. A device that connects the computer and a telephone line. It converts signals so that data can be carried along the wires to various locations.

Monitor. The screen that enables viewing of the computer's programs.

Mouse. A device that plugs into the computer, enabling the user to point on the computer screen. The pointer is operated by moving the mouse on the tabletop and clicking with the buttons.

Multimedia. A difficult term to define as there are so many different standards, few of which are rigidly applied. It generally refers to a computer that has a SVGA display and CD-ROM with sound card and speakers.

Optimise. To rearrange files so that the disk will perform at its best speed.

Path. The instruction of the route to be taken to locate files. It will always start with the drive letter and proceed with each directory and sub-directory to reach the destination. Each instruction will be separated by a backslash symbol.

Peripheral. Any device plugged into the system unit, eg printer, scanner, keyboard etc.

PIM (personal information manager). A program that enables the user to keep a collection of personal records such as appointments, telephone numbers, addresses, etc.

Portrait. The opposite of landscape. Also referred to as tall.

Printer. A device that enables work created on a computer to be transferred onto paper.

Processor. The main microchip inside the computer that dictates the speed and efficiency of the system.

Programs. Also known as software. Instructions to the computer written in a special language that enables it to carry out the tasks required.

Quick format. The method of wiping clean the contents of a disk just by deleting the FAT (file allocation table) rather than the whole disk, thus fooling the disk into thinking it has no information stored on it.

Qwerty. A type of keyboard layout named after the first six keys on the top row.

Ram. Random access memory. Usually refers to the memory fitted to the motherboard and used by the CPU but may also refer to memory fitted to certain expansion cards, eg scanner or display cards. Generally, the more you have the faster the computer can operate.

Root directory. The top level directory. Referred to by a corresponding letter of the drive. It is the main structure supporting sub-directories that form the systematic filing of programs and files.

Scanner. A device that can convert photographs and other artwork and/or text into an electronic format that can be understood and manipulated using an appropriate computer program.

Screen saver. A moving display that activates when the computer keyboard or mouse has not been used for a designated period of time. Initially designed to prevent the screen of the monitor from becoming burned with an image display.

Scroll bar. An implement that appears along the bottom and the right-hand side of a window when there is more information in the window than can be seen in the area given. Allows the user to move up and down and side to side to view the remaining information.

Search engine. A facility available on the Internet to aid searching for topics by typing in key words. It reports back all the possible links available.

Selecting. The technique of highlighting text or objects in order to perform a task with them.

Shareware. The distribution of programs on a try-before-you-buy basis.

Software. Programs that can be installed onto a computer, run from a floppy disk or CD-ROM.

Sound card. A circuit board that is fixed inside the computer to enable the playing of sound.

Source drive. The drive on which the information you wish to copy is held.

Surfing the Net. Searching through and viewing the millions of topics available on the World Wide Web.

System file. A file that the computer must have in order for it to function. It tells the computer how to interpret commands issued through the operating system.

Task bar. The bar at the bottom of a Windows 95 screen displaying open programs.

Glossary

Title bar. A bar at the top of a window that has the name of the program/file that is presently selected.

Tool bar. An area that displays graphic icons, enabling quicker access to commands by clicking on them as opposed to searching through the menu options.

Tree. A graphic representation of a disk's directory structure.

Volume label. An identification label given to a disk during formatting. Sometimes used by programs to identify which disk is needed next during an installation.

Wallpaper. The decoration of patterns and colours that can be displayed on the desktop within the Windows program. These will usually be covered up by a program once it is activated.

Window. A box on the computer screen that displays information in a user-friendly way.

Windows (3.11, 95/98). A program which allows information to be displayed on the screen in a graphic way, enabling the user to work easily by finding their way through menus and windows.

Wizard. Assists you to produce a document quickly, using pre-formed layouts with individual touches thrown in.

Word wrapping. Enables text to flow from one line to another automatically as it is entered. In desktop publishing it also means to 'wrap' text around an object or graphic.

WWW (World Wide Web). A collection of on-line documents that are kept and accessed on Internet servers around the world.

Wysiwyg. Standards for 'what you see is what you get', pronounced wizzywig meaning that how a document appears on the screen is how it will look like if it is printed out.

Further Reading

There are many books available for those who wish to become more proficient in some or all areas of computer studies. Most books cover only one subject or program and are quite expensive, so it is wise to think before you buy. Listed are some of the more widely available titles that may be of interest.

The Dummies Series IDG Books. There are dozens of titles in this series covering a wide range of topics and programs. They are written with an amusing and easy reading style, giving a good depth to the subject without getting too technical. Prices vary with titles but are in the region of £18.

Windows 98 Secrets IDG Books. An excellent book for those determined to get the most out of their system. Windows 98 is an extremely complex program that has never been fully documented. This book has over 1,200 pages of help and advice for fine-tuning your system and sorting things out when it all goes wrong. £38.99. ISBN 0-76453-186-7.

Teach Yourself the Internet in 24 hours Sams Publishing. For those who intend to spend time surfing the net, this book explains all about it. It is written in the form of twenty-four one-hour lessons that will take the novice and make them proficient. Well written and easy to follow. £17.95. ISBN 0-672-157521-236-6.

Usborne Computer Series. Specifically for the younger user, these colourfully illustrated books will help children learn more about their computers and the uses to which they can be put. They can also teach the older reader a thing or two. Prices vary.

Peter Norton's Inside the PC Sams Publishing. For the more technically minded who want to know how the computer itself works, this book is excellent. There's not much about a computer that Peter Norton doesn't know – if anything. His diagnostic software and many publications are used by experts throughout the world. This book explains it all in plain English. £26.95.

ISBN 0-672-31041-4.

Seminar-On-A-Disk InfoSource International. An excellent range of tutorials on floppy disk and CD-ROM enabling the user to learn 'hands on'. They cover a wide range of programs and are particularly useful in the business environment. Prices vary, call 0800 318923 for more information.

Useful Addresses

The following companies are recommended by the authors for their products and services.

SYSTEMS, PERIPHERALS AND SOFTWARE

Insight (previously known as Choice Peripherals), Technology Buildings, Highgrounds Way, Worksop, Nottinghamshire S80 3AF. Tel: 0800 073 5735. Competitively priced mail order supplier of a wide range of computer components and software. Web address http://www.insight.com.

Gateway, Clonshaugh Industrial Estate, Dublin 17, Ireland. Tel: 0800 28 2000. Supplier of high quality computer systems with excellent aftersales. Web address http://www.gateway.com/uk.

Evesham Micros, Vale Park, Evesham, Worcestershire WR11 6TD. Tel: 0800 496 0800. Supplier of good quality computer systems. Web address http://www.evesham.com.

Dream Direct, 4 Aristotle Lane, Kingston Road, Oxford OX2 6TY. Tel: 01865 888900. Independent mail order supplier of leisure and learning multi-media software, pre-tested by themselves. E-mail: sales@dream-direct.co.uk.

MAGAZINES AND INTERNET ACCESS

Internet @ccess Made Easy (Paragon Publishing Ltd). Tel: (01202) 299900. Information about the Internet without too many adverts. Bi-monthly, £3.95. Web address http://paragon.co.uk.

Computer Active (VNU Business Publications). Tel: (0171) 316 9000. An excellent beginners' and intermediate users' guide with good projects to follow. Fortnightly, £0.99. Web address http://www.computeractive.co.uk.

Global Internet. Tel: (0870) 909 8023. An Internet Service Provider with reasonable costs and excellent facilities and guidance. Web address http://www/global.net.uk.

The X-Stream Network. Tel: 0870 730 6466. Free Internet access. Web address: http://www.x-stream.com.

Dixons, PC World and Currys. Call into any of the shops for a free CD-ROM that gives free Internet accss to Freeserve. Web address http://www.freeserve.net.

Index

accessories, 37, 46
adding and removing,
    groups, 44, 72
    icons, 44, 72
    menu entries, 58, 65
    programs, 54, 57, 64, 71
alignment, 80
autoexec.bat, 26

bios, 20
bold, 80, 82
boot up, 20, 26

calculator, 37, 46
calendar, 46
cardfile, 46
CD command, 25
CD-ROM, 56
cells, 93
change directory, 25
clicking,
    double, 28
    right, 28
    single, 28
clipart, 124, 134
close, 31, 79
colours, 35, 43
config.sys, 26
control panel, 65
copy and paste, 64, 81, 98
copying, 63, 70, 81
crash, 134

cursor, 28
cut and paste, 63, 81, 98

databases, 103
date, 25, 29
defragmentation, 59
deleting, 64, 72, 81
desktop, 33
desktop publishing, 84
disks, 53
dot matrix, 18
drives, 48, 53

e-mail, 116, 119
exit, 79
Explorer, 61

fields, 104
File Manager, 69
filenames, 49
files, 49, 75, 104
floppy disk, 25, 53
folder, 48
fonts, 80
formatting, 25, 54, 76, 80
formula, 96

games, 46, 111
graphic user interface, 23
GUI, 23

hard disk, 57, 62, 131

help, 38

i-bar, 29
icons, 35, 82
inkjet, 18
Internet, 118

justification, 80

laser, 18
layers, 85

margins, 77
maximise, 31
megabytes, 130
menu system, 29
minimise, 31
modem, 117, 131
mouse, 20, 28
moving, 45, 63
multimedia, 37, 56, 113

new, 77

open, 78
operating system, 18
   DOS, 23
   Windows 3.11, 17, 41, 69
   Windows 95/98, 17, 28, 61
orientation, 77

page set up, 77
Paint, 30
Paintbrush, 46
paste, 81
paths, 48, 50
PIM, 107
printers, 18
printing, 89
processors, 18, 130

PS2, 20

ram, 130
records, 104
recycle bin, 36
reset, 20
restoring, 36
running programs, 29

saving, 43, 56, 78
scandisk, 59
screen saver, 34, 40
scroll bars, 32
setting up
   a page, 77
   a spellchecker, 88
   your desktop, 33
shutting down, 38
software, 13
spellcheck, 88
spreadsheets, 93
surfing, 121
systems, 16

task bar, 29
templates, 85
text, 82
time, 24, 29
tree, 48, 61
typeface, 80

upgrading, 127

wallpaper, 33
web, 120
windows, 30, 33
wizards, 85
word processing, 37, 74, 81
WWW, 120